▶Comprehension Skills

Comprehension B2
Workbook

Siegfried Engelmann • Steve Osborn • Susan Hanner

SRA
McGraw-Hill

Columbus, Ohio

A Division of **The McGraw·Hill** *Companies*

PHOTO CREDITS
Cover Photo: KS Studios

SRA/McGraw-Hill

A Division of The McGraw·Hill Companies

2002 Imprint
Copyright © 1999 by SRA/McGraw-Hill.

Send all inquiries to:
SRA/McGraw-Hill
8787 Orion Place
Columbus, OH 43240-4027

Printed in the United States of America.

ISBN 0-02-674812-6

11 12 13 14   POH   08 07 06 05

A Read the story and answer the questions. Circle the **W** if the question is answered by words in the story, and underline those words. Circle the **D** if the question is answered by a deduction.

> **Your respiratory system brings oxygen, which is a gas in the air, into contact with your blood. When you breathe air in, the air goes down your trachea and into the bronchial tubes in each lung. The bronchial tubes branch off into smaller and smaller tubes. When the air reaches the ends of the bronchial tubes, capillaries in the lungs soak up the oxygen. The oxygen is now in contact with the blood.**

1. What is oxygen?

_____ **W** **D**

2. Where does your respiratory system bring oxygen?

_____

_____ **W** **D**

3. What's the first tube the air goes into?

_____

4. What happens to the bronchial tubes?

_____

_____

5. What happens to the air when it reaches the ends of the bronchial tubes?

_____

_____ **W** **D**

6. Which body system does the oxygen start out in?

_____

7. Which body system does the oxygen end up in?

_____ **W** **D**

B Underline the common part. Circle each sentence that tells **why.** Combine the sentences with **because.**

1. This gold is worth a lot.

   Robbers want this gold.

   _____

   _____

2. Pamela's humerus is broken.

   Pamela's humerus will have to be examined.

   _____

   _____

3. Diana ate carrots.

   Carrots were good for her.

   _____

   _____

4. He is constructing a shack.

He has no residence.

_____

_____

C Fill in each blank.

1. _____

2. _____

3. _____

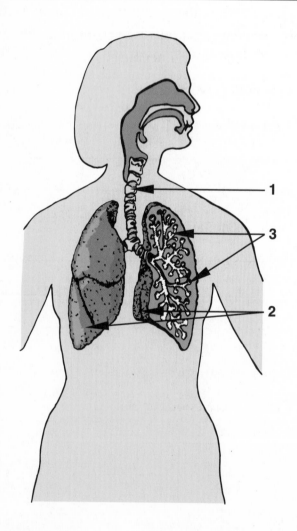

D Tell which fact each statement relates to. Make each contradiction true.

> **1. The ulna is a lower arm bone.**
>
> **2. The man wrote a sentence.**

a. It is moved by the quadriceps. _____

b. It only had a subject. _____

c. It is under the humerus. _____

d. It had an end mark. _____

E Underline the common part. Circle the word that combines the sentences correctly. Combine the sentences with that word.

1. Vince runs every day.

Barbara runs every day.

and   who   which

_____

_____

2. A deer has hooves.

An antelope has hooves.

and   who   which

_____

_____

3. Sandra will run to the store.

Neil will run to the store.

and   who   which

_____

_____

4. Gene resides in that house.

That house is painted white.

and   who   which

_____

_____

5. A strong man lifted Tom.

Tom had a broken leg.

and   who   which

_____

_____

F Tubes that carry blood away from the heart are called

_____.

bronchial tubes   veins   arteries

1. Cross out the word that finishes the sentence correctly.
2. Circle the nouns in the sentence.
3. Above the first noun, write the name of the body system the sentence talks about.
4. Underline the word that means "a pump that moves blood."

G Write a word that comes from **regulate** or **select** in each blank. Then write **verb, noun,** or **adjective** after each item.

1. I don't like traffic _____.

_____

2. He is being very _____ in

filling that job. _____

3. I think her _____ is ugly.

_____

4. They tried to _____ the

cost of cars. _____

H Circle the subject and underline the predicate.

1. My pal Jean broke her femur.
2. Pigs, cows, and horses are all farm animals.
3. Some people have weak hearts.
4. Jumping up and down made the baby tired.
5. The trachea and the lungs are part of the respiratory system.
6. Riding a horse can be very tiring.

A Underline the common part. Circle each sentence that tells **why.** Combine the sentences with **because.**

1. Don needs cash.

   Don is looking for a job.

   _____

   _____

2. Those bushes were too tall.

   Frank cut down those bushes.

   _____

   _____

3. That woman wants to catch fish.

   That woman got some bait.

   _____

   _____

B Complete the instructions.

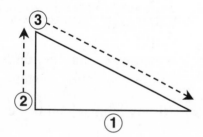

1. Draw a _____

   _____ .

2. Draw a _____ line _____

   from the _____ end of

   the _____ line.

3. Draw a _____ line from the

   _____ of the _____

   _____ to the _____

   _____ of the _____

   _____ .

C Tell which fact each statement relates to. Make each contradiction true.

1. **The biceps bends the arm.**

2. **The lower leg has many arteries.**

a. It covers the femur. _____

b. They carry blood away
   from the heart. _____

c. They are near the
   gastrocnemius. _____

d. It moves the humerus. _____

D Read the story and answer the questions. Circle the **W** if the question is answered by words in the story, and underline those words. Circle the **D** if the question is answered by a deduction.

> You know that the capillaries in your lungs soak up oxygen from the air in your bronchial tubes. After the air loses its oxygen, it soaks up carbon dioxide from the capillaries. When you breathe out, the air goes out your bronchial tubes. This air, which now has carbon dioxide in it, goes up your trachea and out of your nose and mouth. Remember, you breathe in oxygen and you breathe out carbon dioxide.

1. What do the capillaries in your lungs do?

_____

_____

_____ **W** **D**

2. What does the air do after it loses its oxygen?

_____

_____ **W** **D**

3. What does the air soak up from the capillaries?

_____

4. What do the capillaries take from the air?

_____

5. What gas do you breathe in?

_____ **W** **D**

6. What gas do you breathe out?

_____ **W** **D**

7. Which system takes oxygen from the lungs?

_____ **W** **D**

E Write a word that comes from **reside** or **produce** in each blank. Then write **verb, noun,** or **adjective** after each item.

1. Those jobs need _____

people. _____

2. There are many trees in that _____

part of town. _____

3. The boss wants them to _____

more. _____

4. Sam's _____ is too big for

him. _____

F Write the conclusion of each deduction.

1. Burning things need oxygen.
Fires are burning things.

_____

_____

2. Burning things produce carbon dioxide.
Fires are burning things.

_____

_____

3. Arteries carry blood away from the heart.
The aorta is an artery.

_____

_____

G Underline the common part. Circle the word that combines the sentences correctly. Then combine the sentences with that word.

1. Your body needs vitamin A.

Vitamin A comes from carrots.

and who which

_____

_____

2. The skeletal system is made up of bones.

The skeletal system holds up your body.

and who which

_____

_____

3. The player was arguing with the ref.

Her coach was arguing with the ref.

and who which

_____

_____

4. The lungs are part of the respiratory system.

The respiratory system brings oxygen to the blood.

and who which

_____

_____

_____

5. New York is on the East Coast.

Maine is on the East Coast.

and who which

_____

_____

4. Bill criticized his sister.

His sister had been mean.

and who which

_____

_____

H Circle the subject and underline the predicate.

1. Drinking pop is not good for people.

2. The time is three o'clock.

3. To produce films takes a lot of cash.

4. A protective wall kept the fort from harm.

5. Horses and cows eat oats and grass.

6. Riding a bike is good for you.

I Underline the nouns. Draw a line **over** the adjectives. Circle the verbs.

1. Burning things need oxygen.

2. That thermostat is regulating the heat in this room.

3. Some burning things produce heat and smoke.

4. The bronchial tubes are inside the lungs.

A Complete the instructions.

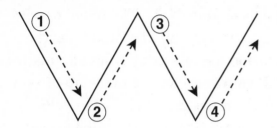

1. Draw a line that _____
_____ _____
_____ _____.

2. Draw a line that _____
_____ _____
_____ _____
from the _____ of line 1.

3. Draw _____ _____
that _____ _____
_____ _____
_____ from the _____
of line 2.

4. Draw a line that _____
_____ _____
_____ _____
from the _____ _____
_____ _____.

B Underline the common part.
If one of the sentences tells **why,**
combine the sentences with **because.** If
neither sentence tells why, combine them
with **who, which,** or **and.**

1. The man went home.

The man ate dinner.

_____

_____

2. The man was hungry.

The man ate dinner.

_____

_____

3. The man rested his legs.

His legs were long.

_____

_____

4. The man rested his legs.

His legs hurt.

_____

_____

5. The man hurt himself.

The man yelled.

_____

_____

C Tell how the things are the same.

1. The man ran like a bullet.

_____

_____

2. The man had a fist like a brick.

_____

_____

3. The woman's hair was like coal.

_____

_____

D Write the middle part of each deduction.

1. Burning things need oxygen.

_____

So, fires need oxygen.

2. Burning things produce carbon dioxide.

_____

So, fires produce carbon dioxide.

3. Some veins carry oxygen.

_____

So, maybe the vena cava carries oxygen.

E Read the story and answer the questions. Circle the **W** if the question is answered by words in the story, and underline those words. Circle the **D** if the question is answered by a deduction.

You know that your circulatory system keeps fresh blood moving to all parts of your body. The blood carries oxygen to all muscles, and it carries carbon dioxide away from all muscles. All your muscles are made up of very small things called cells. The cells, which are like burning things, need oxygen and produce carbon dioxide. If your cells don't get oxygen, you die. If your cells don't get rid of carbon dioxide, you die.

1. What does the circulatory system do?

_____

_____ **W**   **D**

2. What does the blood carry **to** all muscles?

_____ **W**   **D**

3. What does the blood carry **away** from all muscles?

_____ **W**   **D**

4. Are your cells like fire?

_____ **W**   **D**

5. Why?

_____

_____

6. What do your cells make?

_____

7. If a fire goes out, what gas isn't it getting?

_____ **W**   **D**

F Fill in each blank.

1. _____

2. _____

3. _____

4. _____

5. _____

6. _____

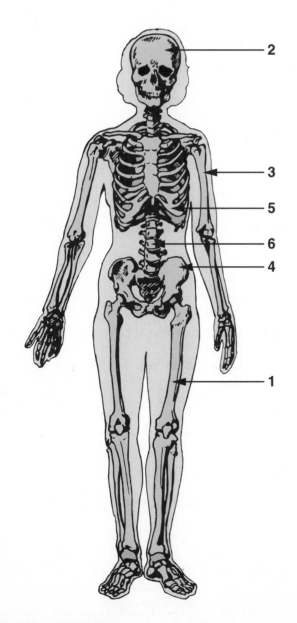

G Circle the subject and underline the predicate.

1. The respiratory system brings oxygen to the blood.

2. Hammers and hoes are tools.

3. To write a book takes lots of time.

4. Jumping down the stairs is not safe.

5. Containers hold things.

6. The abdominal muscle goes from the ribs to the pelvis.

H Write **R** for each fact that is **relevant** to what happened. Write **I** for each fact that is **irrelevant** to what happened.

The doctor looked at the man's lungs.

1. The doctor made lots of cash. _____

2. The man wheezed. _____

3. The man didn't breathe very well. _____

4. The man didn't like the doctor. _____

I Make each statement mean the same thing as the statement in the box.

The digestive system modifies food.

1. The digestive system constructs food.

2. The respiratory system modifies food.

3. The digestive system is a system that changes food.

4. Food is not changed by the digestive system.

A Tell how the things are the same.

1. His dog eats like a pig.

_____

_____

2. His hair grows like weeds.

_____

_____

3. Her lips were like roses.

_____

_____

B Write a word that comes from **modify** in each blank. Then write **verb, noun,** or **adjective** after each item.

1. The digestive system _____

food. _____

2. This new car has many _____.

_____

3. That hot rod is a _____

truck. _____

4. The writer is _____ his

book. _____

5. That book has so many _____

that it is almost new. _____

C Underline the common part. If one of the sentences tells **why,** combine the sentences with **because.** If neither sentence tells why, combine them with **who, which,** or **and.**

1. Linda was thirsty.

Linda drank lots of water.

_____

_____

2. Roberta was thirsty.

Roberta was hungry.

_____

_____

3. That silver is in a box.

Antony protects that silver.

_____

_____

4. That silver is worth a lot.

Ted protects that silver.

_____

_____

5. This cat was running down the street.

A man was running down the street.

_____

_____

D Read the story and answer the questions. Circle the **W** if the question is answered by words in the story, and underline those words. Circle the **D** if the question is answered by a deduction.

> **Your biceps is made up of cells that are like burning things. The carbon dioxide that the cells produce is carried back to the heart by a vein. The blood in this vein is almost black. When the blood gets to the heart, the heart pumps it to the lungs. The heart doesn't change the blood; it just pumps it. The tube that carries the blood from the heart to the lungs is called the pulmonary artery. It is one of the biggest arteries in your body.**

1. What is your biceps made up of?

_____

_____ W   D

2. What gas does the blood carry from the biceps to the heart?

_____ W   D

3. Why is that blood almost black?

_____

_____ W   D

4. What happens to the blood when it gets to the heart?

_____

_____ W   D

5. Does the heart change the blood?

_____

6. What color is blood in the pulmonary artery?

_____

7. Why is the pulmonary artery an artery?

_____

_____

_____ W   D

E Write **R** for each fact that is **relevant** to what happened. Write **I** for each fact that is **irrelevant** to what happened.

> **The woman can't get food to her stomach.**

1. She likes to eat ham.   _____

2. Her esophagus is blocked.   _____

3. She can't open her mouth.   _____

4. She liked her doctor.   _____

F Circle the subject and underline the predicate.

1. Vehicles take things places.

2. To sing well takes practice.

3. Every sentence is divided into two parts.

4. Boxes and paper bags are containers.

5. Making presents can be fun.

6. The skeletal system is made up of bones.

G Tell which fact each statement relates to. Make each contradiction true.

| 1. The stick was burning. |
| 2. The man had a cast on his chest. |

a. It was below the pelvis. _____

b. It was producing oxygen. _____

c. He probably broke his ribs. _____

d. It needed carbon dioxide. _____

H Fill in each blank.

1. _____

2. _____

3. _____

4. _____

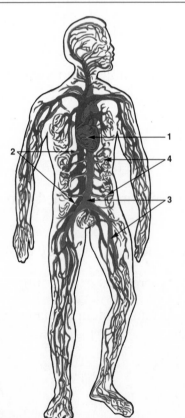

I Follow the directions.

1. Draw a vertical line.
2. Draw a line that slants down to the right from the bottom of the vertical line.
3. Draw a muscle that covers the right side of the vertical line and attaches to the right side of the slanted line.
4. Draw an arrow that shows which way the muscle will move the slanted line.

J Complete the analogies.

1. Tell what system each part is in.

   The heart is to the _____

   _____

   as the lungs are to the _____

   _____.

2. Tell how many of each part you have.

   The heart is to _____

   as the lungs are to _____.

WORD LIST

Abdominal muscle (n) *means* the muscle that goes from the ribs to the pelvis.

Biceps (n) *means* the muscle that covers the front of the humerus.

Criticize (v) *means* find fault with.

Gastrocnemius (n) *means* the muscle that covers the back of the lower leg.

Produce (v) *means* make.

Quadriceps (n) *means* the muscle that covers the front of the femur.

Regulate (v) *means* control.

Regulation (n) *means* a rule.

Regulatory (a) *means* that something regulates.

Residence (n) *means* a place where someone resides.

Selection (n) *means* something that is selected.

Trapezius (n) *means* the muscle that covers the back of the neck.

Triceps (n) *means* the muscle that covers the back of the humerus.

A Underline the common part.
If one of the sentences tells **why,**
combine the sentences with **because.**
If neither sentence tells why, combine
them with **who, which,** or **and.**

1. Fred won the race.

Fred was a fast runner.

_____

_____

2. Fred was a fast runner.

Bob saw Fred.

_____

_____

3. The team lost the game.

The team was sad.

_____

_____

4. The team lost the game.

The game lasted ten innings.

_____

_____

5. The team criticized the coach.

The coach was mean.

_____

_____

B Read the story and answer the questions.
Circle the **W** if the question is answered
by words in the story, and underline
those words. Circle the **D** if the question
is answered by a deduction.

The pulmonary artery carries the
carbon dioxide blood to the lungs. The
lungs take away the carbon dioxide and
put oxygen in its place. When the blood
is filled with oxygen, it goes back to the
heart through the pulmonary vein.
When the blood gets to the heart, the
heart pumps it into an artery called the
aorta. The aorta branches into smaller
and smaller arteries, which carry the
blood to all parts of the body.

1. What color is blood in the pulmonary artery?

_____ **W**   **D**

2. What color is blood in the pulmonary vein?

_____ **W**   **D**

3. Why is blood in the pulmonary vein red?

_____

4. What color is blood in the aorta?

_____ **W**   **D**

5. Why is the aorta an artery?

_____

_____ **W**   **D**

6. What gas does blood in the aorta carry?

_____

C Underline the contradiction. Circle the statement it contradicts.

1. All dogs are called canines. Every dog has warm blood. Some dogs have spotted fur. * Some dogs are brown. Some dogs have cold blood. Most dogs have homes, but some roam the streets.

2. Pam had a race with her older brother. They ran ten blocks. They both wore sneakers. * Pam won the race. Her brother said, "You won because you are older than I am."

D Tell how the things are the same.

1. That man's nose is like a banana.

   _____

   _____

2. Her hands were like sandpaper.

   _____

   _____

3. His eyes are like emeralds.

   _____

   _____

E Fill in each blank.

1. _____

2. _____

3. _____

4. _____

5. _____

6. _____

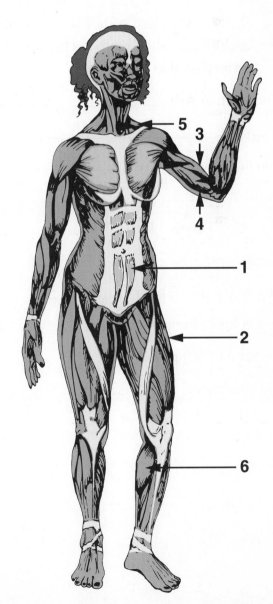

F Underline the nouns.
Draw a line **over** the adjectives.
Circle the verbs.

1. Some arteries have red blood.

2. The man spent his time modifying his car.

3. His car has a modified carburetor.

4. The man modified his carburetor with a wrench.

G Write a word that comes from **modify** in each blank. Then write **verb, noun,** or **adjective** after each item.

1. The woman will _____

    the plane. _____

2. His dad made many _____

    in their residence. _____

3. He said, "People like to _____

    residences." _____

4. His wife said, "These _____

    cost a lot of money." _____

5. So his dad stopped _____

    the residence. _____

H Circle the subject and underline the predicate.

1. Keeping a secret can be hard.

2. School buses and yellow cabs are vehicles.

3. The digestive system changes food into fuel.

4. **Criticize, predict,** and **reside** are verbs.

5. To run in races is thrilling.

6. The esophagus and the trachea are both tubes.

A On your own lined paper, rewrite the paragraph by combining the sentences that are joined with an underline. If one of the sentences tells **why,** combine the sentences with **because.**

Birds make nests. Birds need a place to live. They make their nests from twigs. They make their nests from leaves. It is hard to see some nests. Some nests are hidden in trees.

 B Underline the contradiction. Circle the statement it contradicts.

1. Mr. Jones worked for a car maker. Mr. Jones spent all day at the factory putting on tires. When Mr. Jones came home in the evening, he was too tired to do anything. * He would watch TV all night and yell at the ads. "I would rather do anything than put tires on bikes," Mr. Jones told himself. "I think I'll quit this job and become a thinker."

2. People use their brains to think and feel. If you don't eat the right food when you are a baby, you can suffer damage to your brain. This damage cannot be corrected. Some people don't know this. * They don't feed their babies the right food. When the child grows up, he or she must have an operation to correct the damage. It is very important to eat the right kinds of foods.

 C Tell how the things are the same.

1. Sam's arms are sticks.

_____

_____

2. The room was like a cave.

_____

_____

3. Her smile was like the sun.

_____

_____

D Write **R** for each fact that is **relevant** to what happened. Write **I** for each fact that is **irrelevant** to what happened.

Pam wrote six adjectives in one sentence.

1. She wrote each of these words before a noun. _____

2. The sentence had two verbs. _____

3. She was writing about her dog. _____

4. She was writing at her desk. _____

E Read the story and answer the questions. Circle the **W** if the question is answered by words in the story, and underline those words. Circle the **D** if the question is answered by a deduction.

> **The circulatory system is pretty easy to understand if you remember that the blood does four things. First, it carries carbon dioxide away from the body cells to the heart. Second, it is pumped by the heart to the lungs, where it gives up its carbon dioxide. Third, it gets oxygen from the lungs and goes back to the heart. Fourth, it is pumped by the heart to all parts of the body.**

1. Why do the body cells produce carbon dioxide?

_____

_____

2. What color is blood that goes from the body cells to the heart?

_____ **W**   **D**

3. What gas is carried by blood that goes from the heart to the lungs?

_____

4. What color is blood that goes from the lungs to the heart?

_____ **W**   **D**

5. What gas is carried by blood that goes from the heart to the body cells?

_____

6. What gas does the blood get after it is pumped to the lungs?

_____

7. What kind of tubes carry blood away from the heart?

_____

F Fill in each blank.

1. _____

2. _____

3. _____

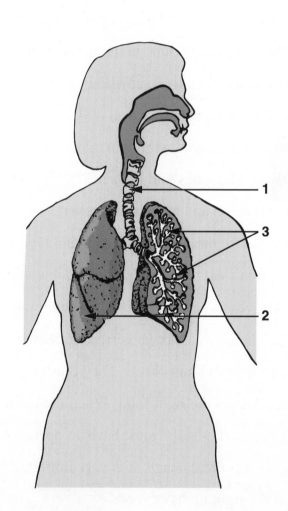

G The —————————— **brings outside air to the lungs.**

1. Finish the sentence.
2. Circle the adjectives.
3. Above the second adjective, write the name of the body system the sentence is talking about.
4. Below the verb, write the verb that means **make**.

H Circle each bone that will move. Then draw an arrow that shows which way it will move.

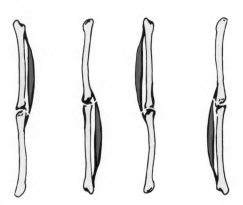

I Underline the nouns. Draw a line **over** the adjectives. Circle the verbs.

1. That float won the contest.

2. His boat will float when that leak is fixed.

3. Three thick logs floated down a slow stream.

4. Most students follow regulations.

ERRORS | O | W | B | T

A

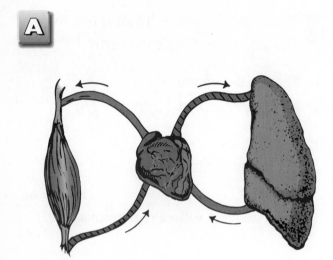

B

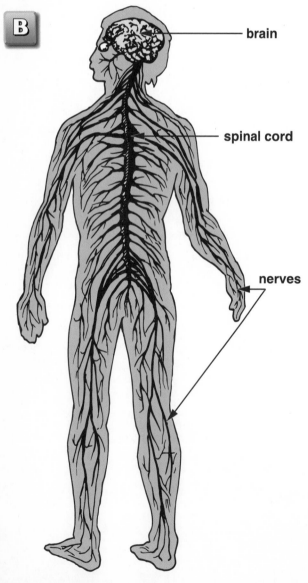

brain

spinal cord

nerves

C On your own lined paper, rewrite the paragraph by combining the sentences that are joined with an underline. If one of the sentences tells **why,** combine the sentences with **because.**

James passed a big test. James was very happy.　The test was in his French class. His French class met in the afternoon.　James spoke French very well. James studied hard.

D Underline the contradiction. Circle the statement it contradicts.

1. Your body is often its own doctor. It can heal itself of many sicknesses. When you are sick, you are weak because your body is in a war with the sickness. If you are not healthy, your body is not in good shape for a war. * Your body cannot heal many things, but it needs to be healthy to heal what it can. Some people heal faster than others. They watch what they eat, and they get lots of sleep.

2. It is very important to learn about money. You will need money if you want a car, if you want to travel, or if you want some shoes. You have to be careful of stores that try to cheat you. * You have to stretch your dollar by looking for the best deals. No one will try to trick you, but you must learn to be smart. The smarter you are about money, the more you will have when you need it.

E Tell **two** ways that the things compared are **not** the same. Tell **one** way that the things compared **are** the **same.**

The man ran like a bullet.

1. A man is not _____

_____.

2. A bullet is not _____

_____.

3. _____

_____

F Complete the instructions.

1. Draw a _____ _____.

2. Draw _____ _____

_____ at the _____ end

of line 1.

3. To _____ _____

_____ _____

_____, write the

_____ that comes from the

verb _____.

4. Below the _____ of line 1,

write the _____ that means

_____.

G Read the story and answer the questions. Circle the **W** if the question is answered by words in the story, and underline those words. Circle the **D** if the question is answered by a deduction.

> The con man was in a place that was very dark when he cut his hand. He could feel it bleeding. He said to himself, "If a bandage stops my hand from bleeding, I know that a vein is bleeding. If a bandage does not stop my hand from bleeding, I know that an artery is bleeding."

1. What color is the blood in the arteries of your hand?

_____

2. What color is the blood in the veins of your hand?

_____

3. Why is the blood in your veins almost black?

_____

_____

4. Which would be harder to stop bleeding, a cut artery or a cut vein?

_____ **W** **D**

5. If the bandage stops the bleeding, what color is the blood that comes out of the cut?

_____ **W**   **D**

6. If the bandage does not stop the bleeding, what color is the blood that comes out?

_____ **W**   **D**

H Draw in the muscles.

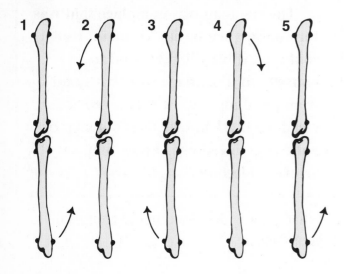

I Write a word that comes from **predict** or **modify** in each blank. Then write **verb, noun,** or **adjective** after each item.

1. The man never bet on _____

games. _____

2. A carpenter will _____ this

home. _____

3. The home needs many _____.

_____

4. The woman's _____ about

the game were wrong. _____

5. _____ a car can cost a lot

of money. _____

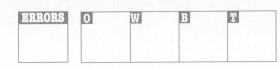

ERRORS | O | W | B | T

A

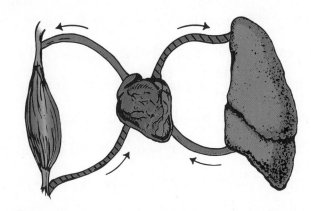

B Read the story and answer the questions. Circle the **W** if the question is answered by words in the story, and underline those words. Circle the **D** if the question is answered by a deduction.

> One of the kids said, "Don't cut yourself. You can't con me with this game, and I'll tell you why. Blood that carries oxygen is red. There is oxygen in the air. When you cut yourself, the oxygen in the air comes into contact with the blood in the cut, and the blood turns red. It doesn't matter if you cut an artery, a vein, or a capillary. The blood will always turn red. Don't try to con me anymore."

1. What color is blood that carries carbon dioxide?

_____

2. What color is blood that carries oxygen?

_____

3. What is one gas in the air?

_____ W   D

4. What color will blood turn if you put it in the air?

_____ W   D

5. Why? _____

_____

_____ W   D

6. If there is no oxygen in the air, will the blood be red when you cut yourself?

_____ W   D

C Tell **two** ways that the things compared are **not** the same. Tell **one** way that the things compared **are** the same.

Their hair grows like weeds.

1. _____

_____

2. _____

_____

3. _____

_____

LESSON 8

D Underline the common part. Then combine the sentences with **who** or **which.**

1. John lifts big boxes.

   John has strong biceps.

   _____

   _____

2. The stomach is under the heart.

   The stomach mixes food.

   _____

   _____

3. The biceps moves the lower arm.

   The biceps pulls like a rubber band.

   _____

   _____

   _____

4. The heart pumps blood.

   The heart is in the circulatory system.

   _____

   _____

   _____

E Underline the contradiction. Circle the statement it contradicts.

Only some people like team sports. Other people like sports that they can do alone, like running. When you play on a team, you must depend on other people and work together. * When you run, you train yourself and depend on yourself. Although everyone likes team sports, single sports can be thrilling. Most track events are single sports, and the greatest of them all is the marathon.

F Write what each analogy tells.

What burning things do to each gas
What color blood is that carries each gas
Where you find each gas
What your respiratory system does to each gas

1. Oxygen is to need as carbon dioxide is to produce.

   _____

   _____

2. Oxygen is to breathing in as carbon dioxide is to breathing out.

   _____

   _____

3. Oxygen is to red as carbon dioxide is to almost black.

_____

_____

G Complete the instructions.

predictable ④   modify ③

1. Draw _____ _____

_____.

2. Draw a line that _____

_____ _____

_____ _____ from

the _____ of the

first line.

3. To the _____ of line 2, write the verb that means _____.

4. Write the _____ that comes

from the verb _____

to the left of the line.

H Circle the subject and underline the predicate.

1. Blood that carries oxygen is red.

2. Gray whales and snakes are animals.

3. Blood that carries carbon dioxide is almost black.

4. To laugh at jokes is human.

5. Verbs tell the action that things do.

6. The muscular system is made up of muscles.

I Write the middle part of each deduction.

1. Blood that carries carbon dioxide is black.

_____

_____

So, blood in the arm veins is black.

2. Blood that carries oxygen is red.

_____

So, blood in the aorta is red.

3. Arteries carry blood away from the heart.

_____

So, the aorta carries blood away from the heart.

J In each blank write the word that has the same meaning as the word or words under the blank.

1. The skull _____ your brain.
(guards)

2. The new cars have many _____.
(changes)

3. She got glasses after her eyes were

_____.
(looked at)

4. My _____ for lunch was french fries.
(choice)

ERRORS | O | W | B | T

A Underline the contradiction.
Circle the statement it contradicts.

Sam was running in a track meet. He hurt the muscle in his lower leg. He won the race, but he had to go to the doctor. * The doctor looked at his leg and shook his head. "You hurt your quadriceps," he said. "You won't be able to run for a while." He taped up Sam's lower leg and gave Sam some crutches.

B Underline the common part. Then combine the sentences with **who** or **which.**

1. The lungs bring fresh air to the blood.
   The lungs are large organs.

   _____

   _____

2. Pam makes boats.
   Pam is very productive.

   _____

   _____

3. This button regulates the heat.
   This button is yellow.

   _____

   _____

4. That doctor plays the trumpet.

   That doctor examined my femur.

   _____

   _____

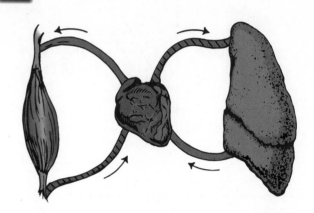

D Write a word that comes from **digest** or **conclude** in each blank. Then write **verb, noun,** or **adjective** after each item.

1. She made a prediction about the

   _____ of the play. _____

2. The _____ system changes food

   into fuel. _____

3. Tom is _____ his

   comments now. _____

4. Her doctor made some _____

   remarks. _____

5. _____ is important to your body.

   _____

E Write **brain, nerves,** or **spinal cord** in each blank.

1. _____

2. _____

3. _____

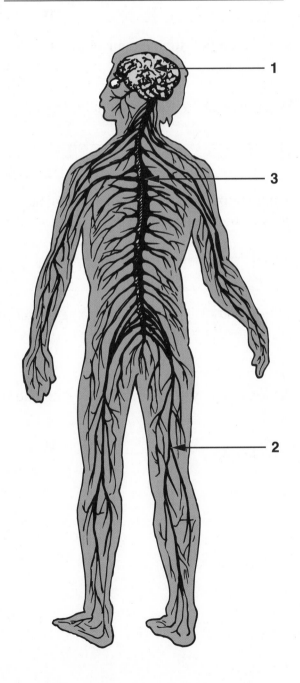

F Tell **two** ways that the things compared are **not** the same. Tell **one** way that the things compared **are** the same.

Their arms are sticks.

1. _____

_____

2. _____

_____

3. _____

_____

G Write the conclusion of each deduction.

1. Blood that carries oxygen is red.
Blood in the aorta carries oxygen.

_____

_____

2. Blood that carries carbon dioxide is almost black.
Blood in the arm veins carries carbon dioxide.

_____

_____

3. Veins carry blood back to the heart.
The vena cava is a vein.

_____

_____

Follow the directions.

1. Draw a horizontal line.
2. Draw a line that slants down to the left from the left end of the horizontal line.
3. Draw a muscle that covers the bottom of the horizontal line and attaches to the right side of the slanted line.
4. Circle the line that will move.

Read the story and answer the questions. Circle the **W** if the question is answered by words in the story, and underline those words. Circle the **D** if the question is answered by a deduction.

> Your respiratory system brings oxygen, which is a gas in the air, into contact with your blood. When you breathe air in, the air goes down your trachea and into the bronchial tubes in each lung. The bronchial tubes branch off into smaller and smaller tubes. When the air reaches the ends of the bronchial tubes, capillaries in the lungs soak up the oxygen. The oxygen is now in contact with the blood.

1. What is oxygen?

   _____ **W**   **D**

2. Where does your respiratory system bring oxygen?

   _____

   _____ **W**   **D**

3. What's the first tube the air goes into?

   _____

4. What happens to the bronchial tubes?

   _____

   _____

5. What happens to the air when it reaches the ends of the bronchial tubes?

   _____

   _____ **W**   **D**

6. Which body system does the oxygen start out in?

   _____

7. Which body system does the oxygen end up in?

   _____ **W**   **D**

J Circle the subject and underline the predicate.

1. **Cloud, cup,** and **book** are nouns.

2. Finding money is always fun.

3. The skull and the ribs are protective bones.

4. Constructive criticism is important to some people.

5. To run in school is not a good idea.

6. The circulatory system keeps fresh blood moving in your body.

WORD LIST

Adjective (n) *means* a word that comes before a noun and tells about the noun.

Carbon dioxide (n) *means* a gas that burning things produce.

Construct (v) *means* build.

Constructive (a) *means* that something is helpful.

Modification (n) *means* a change.

Modified (a) *means* that something is changed.

Modify (v) *means* change.

Noun (n) *means* a word that names a person, place, or thing.

Obtain (v) *means* get.

Oxygen (n) *means* a gas that burning things need.

Predict (v) *means* say that something will happen.

Predictable (a) *means* that something is easy to predict.

Regulate (v) *means* control.

Regulatory (a) *means* that something regulates.

Verb (n) *means* a word that tells the action that things do.

ERRORS	O	W	B	T

A Underline the common part. Then combine the sentences with **who** or **which.**

1. The trachea brings air to the lungs.

The trachea is a tube.

_____

_____

2. Tina does not like criticism.

Tina likes to play sports.

_____

_____

3. The quadriceps covers the front of the femur.

The quadriceps is in the muscular system.

_____

_____

_____

4. That old man resides on a farm.

That old man sells milk.

_____

_____

B Shade in each tube that carries dark blood. Tell if each tube is a **vein** or an **artery.**

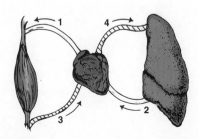

1. _____

2. _____

3. _____

4. _____

C On your own lined paper, rewrite the paragraph by combining the sentences that are joined with an underline. If one of the sentences tells **why,** combine the sentences with **because.**

Bill wanted to skate at the pond. Bill had red hair.   He obtained a pair of skates from his pal. His pal was named Ted.   But Bill did not get to skate at the pond. The pond was not frozen.

D Complete the instructions.

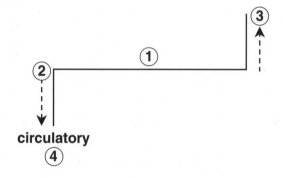

circulatory

1. Draw a _____ _____.

2. Draw a _____ _____

down from the _____

_____ of line 1.

3. Draw a _____ _____

up from the _____

_____ of line 1.

4. Write the word _____

_____ the lower

_____ line.

E Write **brain, nerves,** or **spinal cord** in each blank.

1. _____

2. _____

3. _____

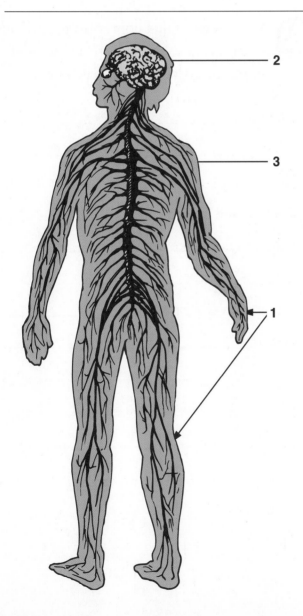

F Tell **two** ways that the things compared are **not** the same.
Tell **one** way that the things compared **are** the same.

Her hands were velvet.

1. _____

_____

2. _____

_____

3. _____

_____

G Underline the contradiction.
Circle the statement it contradicts.

Jim took a class on how to fix engines. He remembered everything that was irrelevant, and he forgot everything that was relevant. When he went to fix his car engine, Jim didn't know what to do. * He said, "Why can't I fix this engine? I remember everything that helps to explain engines." Finally, Jim took his car to a garage, where mechanics fixed his engine for him.

H Read the story and answer the questions. Circle the **W** if the question is answered by words in the story, and underline those words. Circle the **D** if the question is answered by a deduction.

> You know that the capillaries in your lungs soak up oxygen from the air in your bronchial tubes. After the air loses its oxygen, it soaks up carbon dioxide from the capillaries. When you breathe out, the air goes out your bronchial tubes. This air, which now has carbon dioxide in it, goes up your trachea and out of your nose and mouth. Remember, you breathe in oxygen and you breathe out carbon dioxide.

1. What do the capillaries in your lungs do?

   _____

   _____

   _____ **W**   **D**

2. What does the air do after it loses its oxygen?

   _____

   _____ **W**   **D**

3. What do the capillaries give to the air?

   _____

4. What do the capillaries take from the air?

   _____

5. What gas do you breathe in?

   _____ **W**   **D**

6. What gas do you breathe out?

   _____ **W**   **D**

7. Which system takes oxygen from the lungs?

   _____ **W**   **D**

I Write a word that comes from **conclude** or **digest** in each blank. Then write **verb, noun,** or **adjective** after each item.

1. The body _____ food slowly. _____

2. Lin gave _____ proof that Tom ate the cake. _____

3. Rick did not make the right _____.

   _____

4. The mouth is part of the _____ system. _____

5. Your body _____ some foods faster than others. _____

A Write **brain, nerves,** or **spinal cord** in each blank.

1. _____

2. _____

3. _____

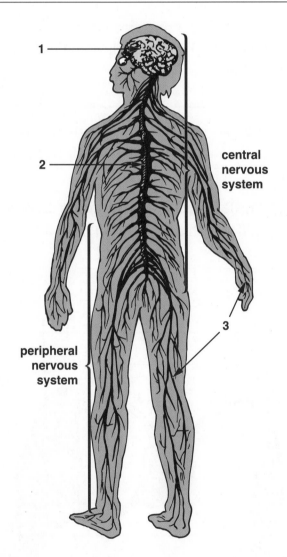

1

2 — central nervous system

3

peripheral nervous system

B On your own lined paper, rewrite the paragraph by combining the sentences that are joined with an underline. If one of the sentences tells **why,** combine the sentences with **because.**

The muscular system does many jobs. The muscular system is made up of muscles. The biceps moves the lower arm. The triceps moves the lower arm. The quadriceps moves the lower leg. The lower leg is very heavy. The fingers have many bones. Tiny muscles move the fingers.

C Underline the common part. Then combine the sentences with **who** or **which.**

1. Mr. Jones gave Jane some criticism.

   Mr. Jones is smart.

   _____

   _____

2. That story is too predictable.

   That story goes on forever.

   _____

   _____

3. The heart is connected to veins and arteries.

   The heart pumps blood.

   _____

   _____

4. A tall basketball player selected three CDs.

   A tall basketball player likes hot tunes.

   _____

   _____

D Read the story and answer the questions. Circle the **W** if the question is answered by words in the story, and underline those words. Circle the **D** if the question is answered by a deduction.

> **Your brain has three parts: the cerebrum, the cerebellum, and the medulla. The cerebrum, which is by far the largest part, takes up the top half of your skull. It is the part that lets you think and feel. The cerebellum, which is under the back part of the cerebrum, regulates your muscular system. The medulla, which is the smallest part, is at the top of the spinal cord. It controls your digestive, circulatory, and respiratory systems.**

1. Name the three parts of your brain.

_____

_____

2. Which part is the smallest?

_____

3. Where is the cerebrum?

_____

_____

4. What does the cerebellum do?

_____

_____ **W**   **D**

5. Where is the cerebellum?

_____

_____ **W**   **D**

6. Which part do you use when you make a deduction?

_____ **W**   **D**

7. Which part regulates your heartbeat?

_____ **W**   **D**

E Shade in each tube that carries dark blood. Tell if each tube is a **vein** or an **artery.**

1. _____

2. _____

3. _____

4. _____

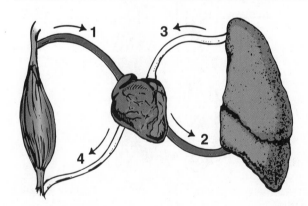

F Tell which fact each statement relates to. Make each contradiction true.

> **1. The cell needed oxygen.**
> **2. The cell was part of the biceps.**

a. It was like a burning thing. _____

b. It was in the lower leg. _____

c. It was a muscle cell. _____

G Tell **two** ways that the things compared are **not** the same.
Tell **one** way that the things compared **are** the same.

> **His shirt was like Swiss cheese.**

1. _____

   _____

2. _____

   _____

3. _____

   _____

H Write the conclusion of each deduction.

1. Burning things produce carbon dioxide. Fires are burning things.

_____

_____

2. Blood that is red carries oxygen. Blood in the arm arteries is red.

_____

_____

3. Some bones protect body parts. The clavicle is a bone.

_____

_____

I Complete the instructions.

1. Draw a _____ _____.

2. Draw a line that _____

   _____ _____

   _____ _____ from

   the _____ of line 1.

3. Draw a _____ that covers the

   right side of line 1 and attaches to the _____

   _____ of line 2.

4. Draw an _____ that shows which

   way _____ _____

   will _____ line 2.

J Write a word that comes from **reside** or **produce** in each blank. Then write **verb, noun,** or **adjective** after each item.

1. Pam _____ in the woods all

summer. _____

2. This factory is more _____

now. _____

3. Pete is afraid to _____ in

that house. _____

4. The _____ part of town is

on a hill. _____

5. New machines may increase _____.

_____

K Fill in each blank.

1. _____

2. _____

3. _____

4. _____

5. _____

6. _____

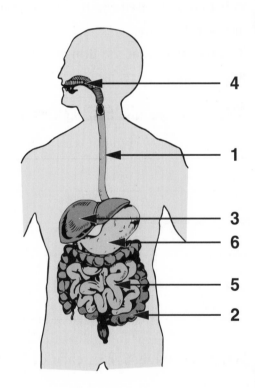

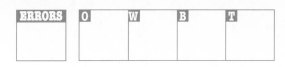

A Write the instructions.

vein ———————— artery
② ① ③

1. (what) _____

_____

2. (what and where) _____

_____

_____

3. (what and where) _____

_____

_____

B Write **brain, spinal cord, nerves, central,** or **peripheral** in each blank.

1. _____

2. _____

3. _____

1 and 2. _____ nervous system

3. _____ nervous system

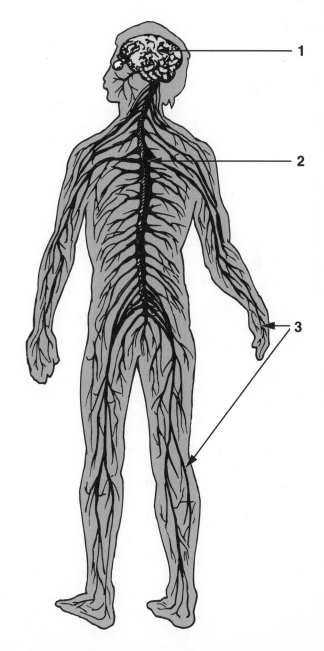

LESSON 12

C Circle the common part that is at the **beginning** of two sentences. Then combine those sentences with **who** or **which.**

1. Tom has black hair.

   Tom is a football player.

   Black hair is good-looking.

   _____

   _____

2. The woman rode her spotted horse.

   Her spotted horse was eating oats.

   Her spotted horse is named Pinto.

   _____

   _____

   _____

3. A big cat digested its food.

   Its food was all meat.

   A big cat sat in the sun.

   _____

   _____

4. That construction is very old.

   That construction has many offices.

   Many offices are always hot.

   _____

   _____

   _____

D Write the middle part of each deduction.

1. Burning things need oxygen.

   _____

   So, fires need oxygen.

2. Blood that is almost black carries carbon dioxide.

   _____

   _____

   So, blood in the leg veins carries carbon dioxide.

3. Some arteries carry carbon dioxide.

   _____

   So, maybe the hepatics carry carbon dioxide.

E Shade in each tube that carries dark blood. Tell if each tube is a **vein** or an **artery.**

1. _____

2. _____

3. _____

4. _____

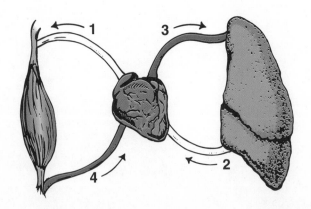

F Tell which fact each statement relates to. Make each contradiction true.

> 1. **The nerve went from the spinal cord to the quadriceps.**
> 2. **The vein went from the quadriceps to the heart.**

a. It was part of the central nervous system. _____

b. It was carrying oxygen. _____

c. It looked almost black. _____

G Tell **two** ways that the things compared are **not** the same.
Tell **one** way that the things compared **are** the same.

> **His back is like a pole.**

1. _____
_____

2. _____
_____

3. _____
_____

H Complete the analogies.

1. Tell which bone each nerve is near.

A biceps nerve is to the _____ as a spinal cord nerve is to the _____.

2. Tell which small system each nerve belongs to.

A biceps nerve is to the _____ _____ as a spinal cord nerve is to the _____.

3. Tell which big system each nerve belongs to.

A biceps nerve is to the _____ _____ as a spinal cord nerve is to the _____.

I Write a word that comes from **protect** or **criticize** in each blank. Then write **verb, noun,** or **adjective** after each item.

1. Those people put up a _____ fence. _____

2. Some chemicals _____ plants from bugs. _____

3. His _____ talk helped me. _____

4. The man made many _____ of the new play. _____

5. These locks will give you extra _____. _____

J Read the story and answer the questions. Circle the **W** if the question is answered by words in the story, and underline those words. Circle the **D** if the question is answered by a deduction.

> **Your cerebrum, which is the most important part of your brain, is divided into two parts. The right side is called the right hemisphere and the left side is called the left hemisphere. In most people the right hemisphere feels and the left hemisphere thinks. When you see, hear, smell, or feel something, you use your right hemisphere. When you think about what you see, hear, smell, or feel, you use your left hemisphere. When you solve a problem or make a deduction, you use your left hemisphere. You often use both hemispheres at the same time. When you read, your right hemisphere sees the words and your left hemisphere thinks about what they mean. When you feel sandpaper, your right hemisphere feels the scratchiness and your left hemisphere concludes that it is sandpaper.**

1. What are the two parts of the cerebrum?

_____

_____

2. What does the right hemisphere do?

_____ **W**   **D**

3. What does the left hemisphere do?

_____ **W**   **D**

4. Tell which hemisphere you would use to do the following things:
a. Think about a story

_____

b. Look at something

_____

c. Smell something

_____

d. Solve a math problem

_____

5. Tell if you use your right hemisphere or both hemispheres:
a. Hearing a question

_____

b. Hearing a question and answering it

_____

c. Smelling something

_____

d. Smelling something and thinking it is a hamburger

_____

A Write the instructions.

①
②
bronchial
③

1. (what) _____
_____

2. (what and where) _____
_____
_____

3. (what and where) _____
_____
_____

B Circle the common part that is at the **beginning** of two sentences. Then combine those sentences with **who** or **which.**

1. A crabby senator concluded his speech.

His speech was long.

His speech had many clever phrases.

_____
_____

2. Those regulations are in six big books.

Six big books are on that shelf.

Those regulations were written by a woman.

_____
_____
_____

3. Carbon dioxide is a gas in the air.

Burning things produce carbon dioxide.

Burning things need oxygen.

_____
_____

4. His uncle wrote books about shells.

Shells can be found in many different places.

His uncle resided near the sea.

_____
_____

C Underline the nouns. Draw a line **over** the adjectives. Circle the verbs.

1. Cats were digesting their food on the porch.

2. The film had a strange conclusion.

3. His friends went to the park after dark.

4. The dark room is scaring that young baby.

D Read the story and answer the questions. Circle the **W** if the question is answered by words in the story, and underline those words. Circle the **D** if the question is answered by a deduction.

> When you walk, your body is doing thousands of things every minute. Your heart is beating; your leg muscles are pulling; your blood is moving. If your cerebrum had to think about doing all those things, it wouldn't have much time for anything else. This is why you have the cerebellum and the medulla. They regulate all the body parts you never think about. The cerebellum controls the muscular system. The medulla controls the digestive, circulatory, and respiratory systems.

1. When you walk, your heart is beating, your leg muscles are pulling, and your blood is moving. Name three other things that your body is doing.

   _____

   _____

   _____

   _____

2. Why doesn't your cerebrum think about all those things?

   _____

   _____

   _____ **W**   **D**

3. Which system does the cerebellum regulate?

   _____ **W**   **D**

4. Which systems does the medulla regulate?

   _____

   _____ **W**   **D**

5. Tell which part of the brain you use for the following things:

   a. bending arm _____

   b. reading _____

   c. listening to the radio _____

   d. running _____

   e. pumping blood _____

E Write **brain, nerves, spinal cord, central,** or **peripheral** in each blank.

1. _____

2. _____

3. _____

1 and 2. _____ nervous system

3. _____ nervous system

F Make each statement mean the same thing as the statement in the box.

Your brain regulates everything your body does.

1. All the things you do are controlled by your brain.

2. Your brain is controlled by all the things your body does.

3. Your body is regulated by your brain.

4. Your body controls your brain.

G Fill in each blank with the word that has the same meaning as the word or words under the blank.

1. Fish _____ oxygen from water.
   (get)

2. He was _____ after the wreck.
   (looked at)

3. The heart _____ the circulatory system.
   (controls)

4. You should _____ your food with care.
   (choose)

H Shade in each tube that carries dark blood. Tell if each tube is a **vein** or an **artery**.

1. _____

2. _____

3. _____

4. _____

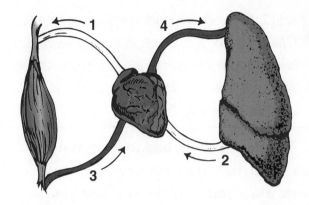

I Circle the subject and underline the predicate.

1. The brain and the spinal cord make up the central nervous system.

2. Running in the cold can be painful.

3. Stores sell many useful products.

4. Burning things produce carbon dioxide.

5. To make a recording is thrilling.

6. Some nerves let you feel.

J Tell **two** ways that the things compared are **not** the same.
Tell **one** way that the things compared **are** the same.

Her eyes were like lights.

1. _____

   _____

2. _____

   _____

3. _____

   _____

ERRORS | O | W | B | T

A Read the story and answer the questions. Circle the **W** if the question is answered by words in the story, and underline those words. Circle the **D** if the question is answered by a deduction.

> **Your cerebellum had to learn how to work, but your medulla knew how to work when you were born. When you first started walking, your cerebrum had to think about every move you made with your walking muscles. As you became better at walking, your cerebellum took over more and more control of those walking muscles. Now you don't have to think about how to walk. The same thing happens every time you learn to do something new with your muscular system, such as playing basketball, dancing, or riding a bike. Your cerebrum controls things at first, but when you have learned how to move your muscles, your cerebellum takes over.**

1. What are the three parts of the brain?

_____

_____

2. What does your cerebellum have to learn?

_____ **W**   **D**

3. Which part controls the walking muscles at first?

_____ **W**   **D**

4. Which part controls the walking muscles later?

_____ **W**   **D**

5. Tell which part of the brain you use for the following things:

a. jumping _____

b. learning how to jump _____

c. thinking _____

d. doing sit-ups _____

e. making a deduction _____

f. rolling over _____

B Circle the common part that is at the **beginning** of two sentences. Then combine those sentences with **who** or **which.**

1. The brain is part of the central nervous system.

The central nervous system includes the spinal cord.

The brain lets you think and feel.

_____

_____

_____

2. The biceps does not move the humerus.

The humerus is part of the skeletal system.

The humerus is in the upper arm.

_____

_____

3. His older sister ran around the block.

His older sister has track shoes.

The block was very big.

_____

_____

4. The man's dog was chasing a cat.

A cat had black fur.

The man's dog had brown feet.

_____

_____

_____

C Write the instructions.

vein _____ · artery
② ① ③

1. (what) _____

_____

2. (what and where) _____

_____

_____

3. (what and where) _____

_____

_____

D Underline the common part. Circle the word that combines the sentences correctly. Combine the sentences with that word.

1. Sir Isaac Newton discovered many things.

Sir Isaac Newton was born in 1642.

because   who   which

_____

_____

_____

2. His dog has brown fur.

Her cat has brown fur.

and   which   who

_____

_____

3. An elephant digests food very slowly.

A whale digests food very slowly.

which   and   because

_____

_____

4. The liver is part of the digestive system.

The esophagus is part of the digestive system.

because   who   and

_____

_____

_____

5. A man was sitting in the yard.

His wife was sitting in the yard.

and   which   because

_____

_____

E Circle the subject and underline the predicate.

1. The nervous system is made up of the central and the peripheral nervous systems.

2. Plants breathe carbon dioxide.

3. Shoveling snow takes strong muscles.

4. To light the street costs money.

5. Blood that carries oxygen is red.

6. Reside, produce, and **modify** are verbs.

F Underline the contradiction.
Circle the statement it contradicts.

Smoking hurts your circulatory system. The blood can't get pure oxygen from your lungs, because your lungs are full of smoke. The blood gets thick and heavy and can't move around your body very well. * If your circulation is poor, your feet and hands get cold easily. Exercise will help your circulation, and sometimes a warm drink will help also. Anything that makes your blood thicker will help your circulation.

G Draw in the arrows. Tell if each tube is a **vein** or an **artery**.

1. _____

2. _____

3. _____

4. _____

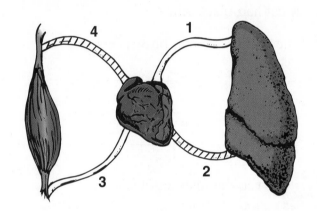

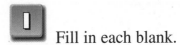

H Write **brain, nerves, spinal cord, central,** or **peripheral** in each blank.

1. _____

2. _____

3. _____

1. _____ nervous system

2 and 3. _____ nervous system

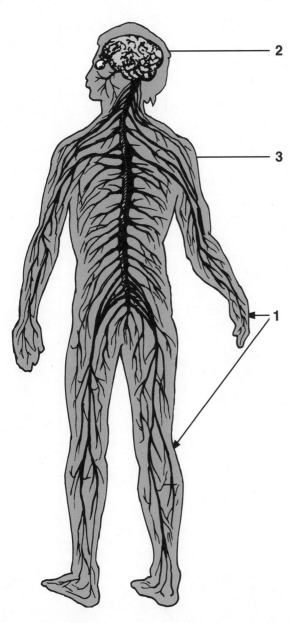

I Fill in each blank.

1. _____

2. _____

3. _____

4. _____

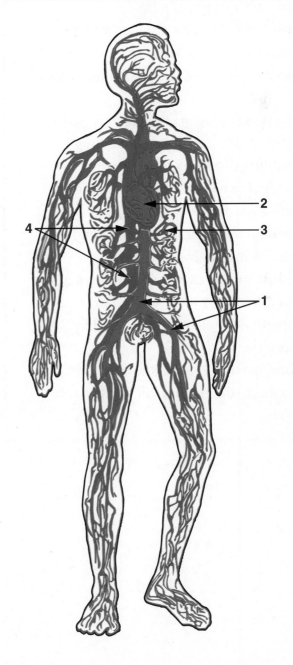

WORD LIST

Brain (n) *means* the organ that lets you think and feel.

Conclude (v) *means* end or figure out.

Conclusion (n) *means* the end or something that is concluded.

Conclusive (a) *means* that something is true without any doubt.

Criticism (n) *means* a statement that criticizes.

Digest (v) *means* change food into fuel for the body.

Digestion (n) *means* the act of digesting.

Digestive (a) *means* that something involves digesting.

Modified (a) *means* that something is changed.

Nerve (n) *means* a wire in the body that carries messages.

Production (n) *means* something that is produced.

Protective (a) *means* that something protects.

Spinal cord (n) *means* the body part that connects the brain to all parts of the body.

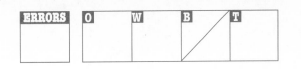

LESSON 15

A Write the instructions.

bronchial
③

1. (what) _____

_____

2. (what and where) _____

_____

_____

3. (what and where) _____

_____

_____

B Circle the common part that is at the **beginning** of two sentences. Then combine those sentences with **who** or **which.**

1. Carbon dioxide turns blood almost black.

Carbon dioxide is a gas in the air.

The air has many other gases.

_____

_____

_____

2. The robber held up Bob's uncle.

Bob's uncle got away from the robber.

Bob's uncle was a cop.

_____

_____

_____

3. Her sentence was about trees.

Trees are her favorite plant.

Her sentence had a long subject.

_____

_____

_____

C Draw in the arrows.
Tell if each tube is a **vein** or an **artery**.

1. _____

2. _____

3. _____

4. _____

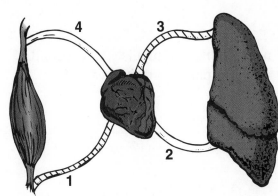

D Read the story and answer the questions. Circle the **W** if the question is answered by words in the story, and underline those words. Circle the **D** if the question is answered by a deduction.

> **When you stub your toe, the message "toe hurts" goes from your toe to your brain. Your nerves don't really carry the words "toe hurts." What they do carry is a little bit of electricity. The electricity comes in very short bursts called impulses. If the toe doesn't hurt too much, the message may have 30 impulses per second. If the toe hurts a lot, the message may have more than 100 impulses per second. The greater the pain, the more impulses per second.**

1. Which system carries the message "toe hurts" to your brain?

   _____ **W**   **D**

2. How is a nerve like a lamp cord?

   _____

   _____ **W**   **D**

3. What are impulses?

   _____

4. If a message has 10 impulses per second, how many impulses will it have in 5 seconds?

   _____

5. Message A has 50 impulses per second. Message B has 120 impulses per second. Which message carries more pain?

   _____ **W**   **D**

6. Which gives more impulses per second: banging your knee against a door or touching your knee with a glove?

   _____

   _____

7. Which gives more impulses per second: touching your finger with a feather or cutting your finger with a knife?

   _____

   _____

E Circle the subject and underline the predicate.

1. Buying new clothes is fun.

2. Burning things need oxygen.

3. Oxygen is needed by burning things.

4. The act of digesting is called digestion.

5. The predicate of a sentence tells more.

6. The nervous system is made up of nerves.

F Write **brain, nerves, spinal cord, central,** or **peripheral** in each blank.

1. _____

2. _____

3. _____

1. _____ nervous system

2 and 3. _____ nervous system

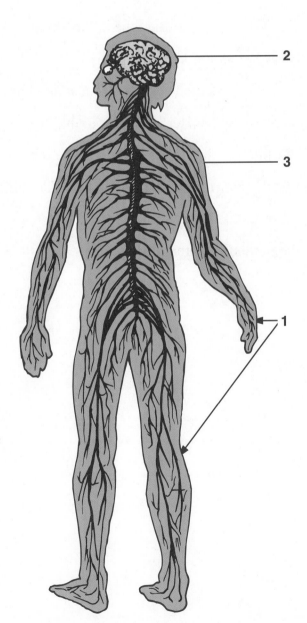

G Fill in each blank.

1. _____

2. _____

3. _____

4. _____

5. _____

6. _____

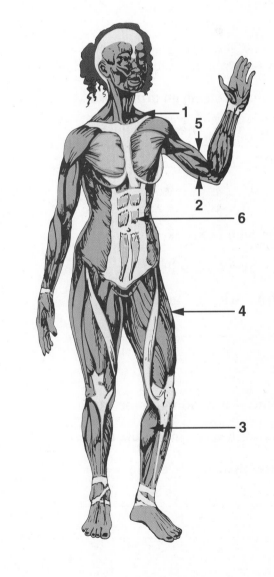

LESSON 15

H Underline the common part. Circle the word that combines the sentences correctly. Combine the sentences with that word.

1. That con man has sold many phony tickets.

His pal has sold many phony tickets.

who   and   which

_____

_____

_____

2. Those women protect an army base.

A man protects an army base.

and   who   because

_____

_____

3. The man was sick.

The man took pills.

who   which   because

_____

_____

4. Sanford was riding in the truck.

His son was riding in the truck.

and   which   because

_____

_____

5. Alabama is in the South.

Mississippi is in the South.

because   and   who

_____

_____

I Underline the contradiction.
Circle the statement it contradicts.

Mary had a sore trachea. She ate lots of ice cream to keep the pain down. She couldn't breathe very well. She wanted to see a doctor. * Her brother took her to the hospital. A doctor there said, "The tubes inside your lungs are hurting you. You will have to take some pills." So Mary went home and took the pills.

A

1. The man was tired by noon.
   By noon, the man was tired.

2. Kids were playing under the table.

   _____

   _____

3. She ate because she was hungry.

   _____

   _____

B   Write the instructions.

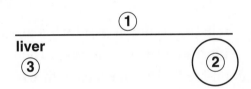

liver

1. (what) _____

   _____

2. (what and where) _____

   _____

   _____

3. (what and where) _____

   _____

   _____

C   On your own lined paper, rewrite the paragraph by combining the sentences that are joined with an underline. If one of the sentences tells **why,** combine the sentences with **because.**

   Muscles need oxygen. Muscles are like burning things.   Muscles can only pull. Muscles are made of things called fibers.   An athlete has very strong muscles. A dancer has very strong muscles.   Any person who exercises a lot will get strong muscles. Strong muscles are good to have.

D   Underline the nouns. Draw a line **over** the adjectives. Circle the verbs.

1. Your arm nerves are in your peripheral nervous system.

2. His mother has many nervous habits.

3. Her conclusion was based on facts.

4. Their criticisms were printed in the newspaper.

LESSON 16

E Fill in each blank.

1. _____

2. _____

3. _____

1. _____ nervous system

2 and 3. _____ nervous system

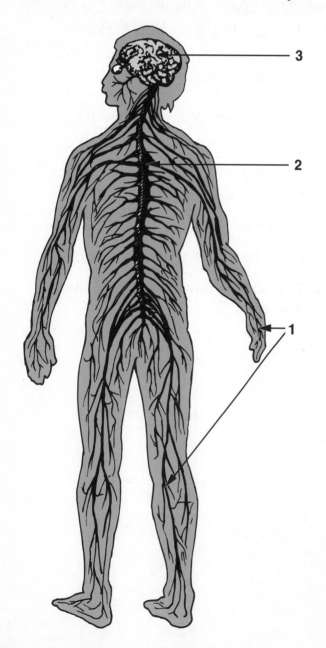

F Fill in each blank with the word that has the same meaning as the word or words under the blank.

1. Don't _____ him until he
           (find fault with)
   makes a mistake.

2. Some _____ don't make sense.
           (rules)

3. If you _____ that coat, you can't
        (change)
   return it.

4. He _____ his
       (changed into fuel for the body)
   lunch.

G Circle the common part that is at the **beginning** of two sentences. Then combine those sentences with **who** or **which.**

1. His older sister's cat had white feet.

   His older sister's cat was named Fats.

   White feet can get very dirty.

   _____

   _____

   _____

2. Dan was very fast.

   The race was long.

   Dan won the race.

   _____

   _____

3. Nerves carry messages.

Messages are made up of electricity.

Nerves are wires.

_____

_____

H Read the story and answer the questions. Circle the **W** if the question is answered by words in the story, and underline those words. Circle the **D** if the question is answered by a deduction.

> **Your biceps is made up of burning cells. The carbon dioxide that the cells produce is carried back to the heart by a vein. The blood in this vein is almost black. When the blood gets to the heart, the heart pumps it to the lungs. The heart doesn't change the blood; it just pumps it. The tube that carries the blood from the heart to the lungs is called the pulmonary artery. It is one of the biggest arteries in your body.**

1. What is your biceps made up of?

_____ **W**   **D**

2. What gas does the blood carry from the biceps to the heart?

_____

3. Why is that blood almost black?

_____

_____ **W**   **D**

4. What happens to the blood when it gets to the heart?

_____

_____ **W**   **D**

5. Does the heart change the blood?

_____

6. What color is blood in the pulmonary artery?

_____

7. Why is the pulmonary artery called an artery?

_____

_____ **W**   **D**

I Write **R** for each fact that is **relevant** to what happened.
Write **I** for each fact that is **irrelevant** to what happened.

The man had a pain in his central nervous system.

1. He had hurt his finger.   _____

2. He had hurt his spinal cord.   _____

3. His toe was over a fire.   _____

4. He had hurt nerves inside his backbone.   _____

LESSON 16

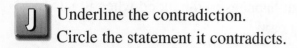

J Underline the contradiction.
Circle the statement it contradicts.

> Bright red blood flowed through a maze of tubes in a scientist's laboratory. Some blood was being heated in flasks. Other blood was getting electrical jolts. The laboratory looked like a jungle. * The scientist said, "I think that blood can be used for many things. This blood has a lot of carbon dioxide. If I get that gas out of the blood, I will sell it to plant stores and make money."

A

a. Underline the common part that is at the **end** of one sentence and the **beginning** of another. Then combine those sentences with **who** or **which.**

b. Circle the common part that is at the **beginning** of two sentences. Then combine those sentences with **who** or **which.**

1. Burning things produce carbon dioxide.

Carbon dioxide is a gas in the air.

Burning things need oxygen.

a. _____

_____

_____

b. _____

_____

_____

2. The biceps bends the arm.

The biceps covers the front of the humerus.

The humerus is the upper arm bone.

a. _____

_____

_____

_____

b. _____

_____

_____

_____

3. Bill had black hair.

John was mad.

Bill listened to John.

a. _____

_____

b. _____

_____

B Write the instructions.

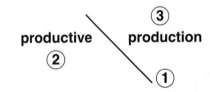

③
productive   production
②   ①

1. (what) _____

_____

2. (what and where) _____

_____

3. (what and where) _____

_____

_____

1. Ann and Jane played ball after school.
After school, Ann and Jane played ball.

2. We can ski if it snows.

3. Dinah went to sleep before ten o'clock.

_____

_____

D Fill in each blank.

1. _____

2. _____

3. _____

4. _____

5. _____

6. _____

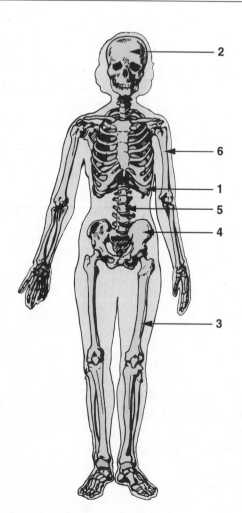

E Fill in each blank.

1. _____

2. _____

3. _____

1 and 3. _____ nervous system

2. _____ nervous system

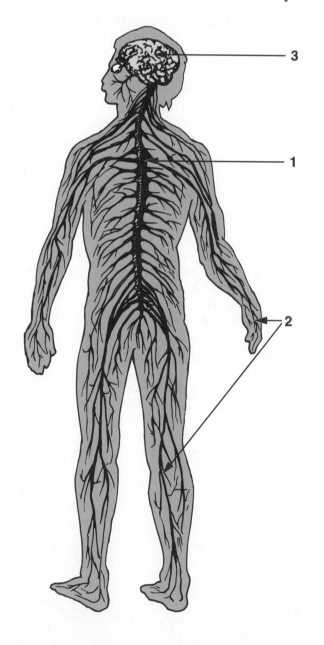

F Make each statement mean the same thing as the statement in the box.

> **The man modified his car because he wanted it to go faster.**

1. The man changed his car so that it would go faster.

2. Because he wanted to make it go faster, the man digested his car.

3. To make it go more quickly, the man changed his car.

4. To make it go faster, the car changed the man.

G Write a word that comes from **reside** or **conclude** in each blank. Then write **verb, noun,** or **adjective** after each item.

1. The people clapped when Bob

_____ his speech.

_____

2. Many snakes _____ in cool

places. _____

3. The _____ of the story was

sad. _____

4. Some _____ areas are for

older people. _____

5. Jim _____ that the power

was off. _____

H Tell **two** ways that the things compared are **not** the same.
Tell **one** way that the things compared **are** the same.

> **The basketball player moved like a rabbit.**

1. _____

_____

2. _____

_____

3. _____

_____

I Draw in the arrows. Shade in each tube that carries dark blood. Tell if each tube is a **vein** or an **artery**.

1. _____

2. _____

3. _____

4. _____

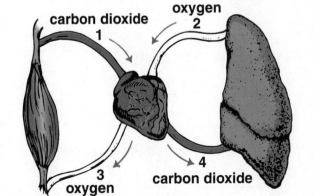

J Read the story and answer the questions. Circle the **W** if the question is answered by words in the story, and underline those words. Circle the **D** if the question is answered by a deduction.

> The pulmonary artery carries the carbon dioxide blood to the lungs. The lungs take away the carbon dioxide and put oxygen in its place. When the blood is filled with oxygen, it goes back to the heart in a vein called the pulmonary vein. When the blood gets to the heart, the heart pumps it into an artery called the aorta. The aorta branches into smaller and smaller arteries, which carry the blood to all parts of the body.

1. What color is blood in the pulmonary artery?

   _____ **W**   **D**

2. What color is blood in the pulmonary vein?

   _____ **W**   **D**

3. Why is blood in the pulmonary vein red?

   _____

4. What color is blood in the aorta?

   _____ **W**   **D**

5. Why is the aorta an artery?

   _____

   _____ **W**   **D**

6. What gas does blood in the aorta carry?

   _____

K Use the rule to answer the questions.

> **The bigger the fire, the more oxygen it needs.**

1. What needs more oxygen, a forest fire or a match?

   _____

2. Hector's fire needed a lot of oxygen. Hank's fire didn't need much oxygen.
   a. Whose fire was bigger?

   _____

   b. How do you know?

   _____

   _____

3. Beverly lit a candle. Susan started a camp fire.
   a. Which person's fire needs less oxygen?

   _____

   b. How do you know?

   _____

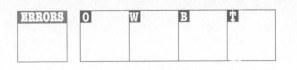

LESSON 18

A

② regulation

①

digestion
③

1. (what) _____

_____

2. (what and where) _____

_____

3. (what and where) _____

_____

B

a. Underline the common part that is at the **end** of one sentence and the **beginning** of another. Then combine those sentences with **who** or **which.**

b. Circle the common part that is at the **beginning** of two sentences. Then combine those sentences with **who** or **which.**

1. The man drank milk.

Milk was good for him.

The man was sick.

a. _____

_____

b. _____

_____

2. The woman was strong.

Her son was crying.

The woman protected her son.

a. _____

_____

_____

b. _____

_____

3. The spinal cord is under the brain.

The spinal cord has many parts.

The brain has many parts.

a. _____

_____

_____

b. _____

_____

_____

C Use the facts to fill out the form.

> **Facts: Your name is James Renton.**
> **Your wife's name is Susan Renton. You**
> **are a police officer who is applying for**
> **a job as a fire fighter. You are now**
> **making $800 a week. Your address is**
> **362 Pleasant Court, Flagstaff, Arizona.**

Instructions:

   a. Enter your name on line 4, last name first.
   b. Write your wife's first name on line 5.
   c. Write the state you live in on line 1.
   d. Write the city you live in on line 2.
   e. On line 3, write how much money you earn each week.
   f. On line 6, write the sentence above that gives information you didn't use in filling out the form.

1. _____
2. _____
3. _____
4. _____
5. _____
6. _____

   _____

D Circle the subject and underline the predicate. Rewrite each sentence by moving part of the predicate.

1. Muscles pull like rubber bands when they work.

   _____

   _____

2. Your respiratory system works hard when you run.

   _____

   _____

   _____

3. The tree looks small next to that house.

   _____

   _____

4. The man went to the store yesterday.

   _____

   _____

E Fill in each blank.

1. _____

2. _____

3. _____

1 and 3. _____ nervous system

2. _____ nervous system

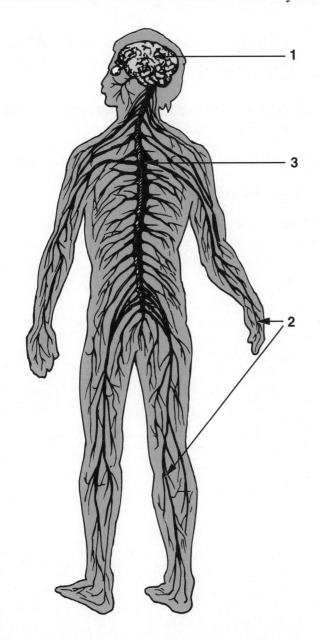

F Write the conclusion of each deduction.

1. Every heart has four chambers.
   Joe has a heart.

   _____

   _____

2. All nerves carry messages.
   The vagus is a nerve.

   _____

3. Some plants produce resin.
   Trees are plants.

   _____

G Tell **two** ways that the things compared are **not** the same.
Tell **one** way that the things compared **are** the same.

The town was like a beehive.

1. _____

   _____

2. _____

   _____

3. _____

   _____

H Underline the common part. Circle the word that combines the sentences correctly. Combine the sentences with that word.

1. Maine is in the Northeast.

Vermont is in the Northeast.

and   who   which

_____

_____

2. Jim always obtains green apples.

Marlene always obtains green apples.

who   and   which

_____

_____

3. New York is one of the oldest states.

New York has lots of people.

who   which   because

_____

_____

4. Oxygen was in the lungs.

Carbon dioxide was in the lungs.

because   who   and

_____

_____

5. Montana is in the Great Plains.

The Dakotas are in the Great Plains.

which   and   because

_____

_____

I Make each statement mean the same thing as the statement in the box.

> **The film concluded with a shot of the sun setting.**

1. A picture of the setting sun was the last shot in the film.

2. The film ended with a picture of the sunset.

3. A sunrise concluded the film.

4. The film started with a sunset.

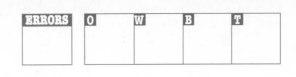

A Write a word that comes from **consume** in each blank. Then write **verb, noun,** or **adjective** after each item.

1. That man _____ too much

   coffee. _____

2. Regulatory agencies try to protect

   _____. _____

3. Cookies are a _____ product.

   _____

4. He can _____ great plates of

   meat. _____

5. Some _____ will buy anything

   that is on sale. _____

B Write the instructions.

modification
③

1. (what) _____

   _____

2. (what and where) _____

   _____

   _____

3. (what and where) _____

   _____

   _____

C Circle the subject and underline the predicate. Rewrite each sentence by moving part of the predicate.

1. People eat lots of fish in Spain.

   _____

   _____

2. He had bacon and eggs for breakfast.

   _____

   _____

3. He modified the car before the race.

   _____

   _____

4. Your digestive system works hard after you eat.

   _____

   _____

   _____

D Use the facts to fill out the form.

> **Facts: Your name is Linda Carlson. You are seventeen years old. You want to be a doctor. You take photographs in your spare time. You earn $100 a week working for the Royal Drug Store. You live at 5642 E. Sixty-third St., Chicago, Illinois.**

Instructions:
a. State your age on line 4.
b. On line 6, tell what kind of job you want to have.
c. On line 3, tell how much money you make in four weeks.
d. On line 2, write the name of the state you live in.
e. Write your first name on line 5.
f. On line 1, write the sentence above that gives information you didn't use in filling out the form.

1. _____

2. _____

3. _____

4. _____

5. _____

6. _____

E Write what each analogy tells.

> **What shape each body part is**
> **What each body part carries**
> **What body system each body part is in**
> **What each body part lets you do**

1. A **nerve** is to the **nervous system** as an **artery** is to the **circulatory system.**

_____

_____

2. A **nerve** is to **feeling** as an **artery** is to **living.**

_____

_____

3. A **nerve** is to **messages** as an **artery** is to **blood.**

_____

_____

F
a. Underline the common part that is at the **end** of one sentence and the **beginning** of another. Then combine those sentences with **who** or **which.**
b. Circle the common part that is at the **beginning** of two sentences. Then combine those sentences with **who** or **which.**

1. The dog consumed pork chops.

The dog resided in a little house.

Pork chops come from pigs.

a. _____

_____

_____

b. _____

_____

_____

2. Jill protects her gold.

Jill examines silver.

Her gold is worth a lot.

a. _____

_____

_____

b. _____

_____

_____

3. Oxygen is needed by the muscles.

The aorta is the biggest artery in the body.

The aorta carries oxygen.

a. _____

_____

_____

b. _____

_____

_____

G Underline the contradiction.
Circle the statement it contradicts.

Plants produce oxygen. Ellen lived in an apartment with lots of plants. The apartment had no windows, and it was very stuffy. * When Ted came to visit Ellen, he noticed all her plants. He said, "The air in your apartment has lots of oxygen." So Ellen opened the window to let new air in.

H Underline the common part. Circle the word that combines the sentences correctly. Combine the sentences with that word.

1. North Carolina was in the Confederacy.

Virginia was in the Confederacy.

which   and   because

_____

_____

2. The blood in your arm veins is dark.

The blood in your arm veins has no oxygen.

who   because   which

_____

_____

3. That swimmer has won many medals.

Her coach has won many medals.

and   who   because

_____

_____

4. The woman put on her swimming suit.

The woman wanted to dive into the lake.

because   and   which

_____

_____

_____

5. New Orleans is south of Chicago.

Memphis is south of Chicago.

and   who   which

_____

_____

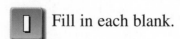 Fill in each blank.

1. _____

2. _____

3. _____

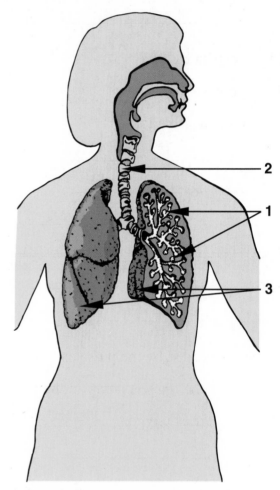

Write the middle part of each deduction.

1. All nerves carry messages.

_____

So, the vagus carries messages.

2. A cat has every kind of blood vessel.

_____

So, a cat has a vein.

3. Some diseases affect the skin.

_____

So, maybe pellagra affects the skin.

WORD LIST

Central nervous system (n) *means* the body system that is made up of the brain and spinal cord.

Conclude (v) *means* end or figure out.

Conclusion (n) *means* the end or something that is concluded.

Conclusive (a) *means* that something is true without any doubt.

Digest (v) *means* change food into fuel for the body.

Examine (v) *means* look at.

Irrelevant (a) *means* that something does not help to explain what happened.

Nervous system (n) *means* the body system of nerves.

Peripheral nervous system (n) *means* the body system that is made up of all the nerves that lead to and from the spinal cord.

Regulation (n) *means* a rule.

Relevant (a) *means* that something helps to explain what happened.

Residential (a) *means* that a place has many residences.

Selective (a) *means* that something is careful about selecting things.

ERRORS | O | W | B | T

A Use the facts to fill out the form.

Facts: Your name is Jim Morgan. You want to open a checking account at the bank. You make $350 a week. Your address is 345 E. Locust St., Ames, Iowa. You work as a janitor for John Jay High School. You are twenty years old. You want a checking account because you don't like carrying cash in your wallet.

Instructions:

a. Write the name of your job on line 3.
b. State your age on line 4.
c. State your weekly income on line 1.
d. Give your street address on line 2.
e. Tell what town you live in on line 6.
f. On line 5, give any reasons you have for opening a checking account.
g. On line 7, write the first sentence above that gives information you didn't use in filling out the form.

1. _____

2. _____

3. _____

4. _____

5. _____

   _____

6. _____

7. _____

   _____

B Write the instructions.

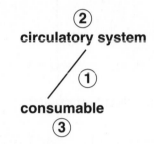

1. (what) _____

   _____

   _____

2. (what and where) _____

   _____

   _____

3. (what and where) _____

   _____

   _____

C Circle the subject and underline the predicate. Rewrite each sentence by moving part of the predicate.

1. It was late when she went to bed.

   _____

   _____

2. Mike paints in his spare time.

   _____

   _____

3. Your nervous system is working when you think or feel.

   _____

   _____

4. We played tennis while the sun was out.

   _____

   _____

D Draw in the arrows. Shade in each tube that carries dark blood. Tell if each tube is a vein or an artery.

1. _____

2. _____

3. _____

4. _____

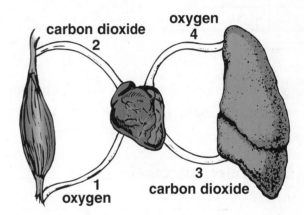

carbon dioxide
2

oxygen
4

1
oxygen

3
carbon dioxide

E On your own lined paper, rewrite the paragraph by combining the sentences that are joined with an underline. If one of the sentences tells **why,** combine the sentences with **because.**

Vitamins are one of the six nutrients. Vitamins can be found in many foods.   Your body needs vitamins. Vitamins help keep you well. Vitamin A is an important vitamin. Vitamin A comes from carrots.   Night blindness is a bad eye disease. Vitamin A can prevent night blindness.

F Write a word that comes from **consume** in each blank. Then write **verb, noun,** or **adjective** after each item.

1. He can't digest the cake he _____.

_____

2. Bob's work _____ all of his

time. _____

3. Wood is a _____ product.

_____

4. Our office _____ a lot of

paper. _____

5. _____ need protection from

some chemicals in food. _____

G Underline the contradiction. Circle the statement it contradicts.

Fred had an accident yesterday. He only hurt nerves in his little toe, but the doctor gave him a big cast. It was hard for Fred to walk with the cast on. * Fred asked the doctor why he needed such a big cast. The doctor said, "Anytime you hurt your central nervous system, you are in big trouble. Be happy that it wasn't any worse."

H a. Underline the common part that is at the **end** of one sentence and the **beginning** of another. Then combine those sentences with **who** or **which.**

b. Circle the common part that is at the **beginning** of two sentences. Then combine those sentences with **who** or **which.**

1. His older brother consumed grapes with zest.

His older brother liked jelly.

Jelly is made from grapes.

a. _____

_____

_____

b. _____

_____

_____

2. His food was very soft.

The man had trouble chewing his food.

The man had no teeth.

a. _____

_____

_____

_____

b. _____

_____

_____

_____

3. His sister played with her cats.

Her cats liked to roll in mud.

His sister liked to roll in mud.

a. _____

_____

_____

b. _____

_____

_____

ERRORS | O | W | B | T

A Use the facts to fill out the form.

Facts: Your name is Anita Anderson. You are applying for a gas credit card. You make $1600 a month. Your rent and heat bills add up to $400 a month. You own a car, which is paid for. You are twenty-five years old. You are a plumber, and you live at 160 Oak St., Danville, Texas.

Instructions:

a. Write your monthly income on line 1.
b. Write the total of your monthly rent and heat bills on line 2.
c. Subtract line 2 from line 1 and write the answer on line 3.
d. State what kind of credit card you want on line 6.
e. Tell your age on line 4.
f. Write your full name, last name first, on line 5.
g. On line 7, write the first sentence above that gives information you didn't use in filling out the form.

1. _____

2. _____

3. _____

4. _____

5. _____

6. _____

7. _____

_____

B Circle the subject and underline the predicate. Rewrite each sentence by moving part of the predicate.

1. Ducks were swimming under the dock.

_____

_____

2. He solved the problem without help.

_____

_____

3. Blood turns dark after its oxygen is used.

_____

_____

4. Apples are ready to eat in the fall.

_____

_____

C Tell what gas each tube carries. Shade in each tube that carries dark blood. Tell if each tube is a vein or an artery.

1. _____

2. _____

3. _____

4. _____

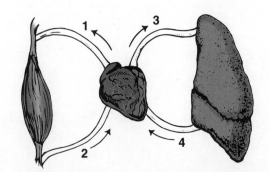

D Tell which fact each statement relates to. Make each contradiction true.

> 1. **The nerve went from the thumb to the spinal cord.**
> 2. **The artery went from the heart to the lungs.**

a. It was part of the peripheral nervous system. _____

b. It was carrying carbon dioxide. _____

c. It carried messages such as "Move thumb." _____

E
a. Underline the common part that is at the **end** of one sentence and the **beginning** of another. Then combine those sentences with **who** or **which.**
b. Circle the common part that is at the **beginning** of two sentences. Then combine those sentences with **who** or **which.**

1. Sense nerves let you feel.

   The brain can do many things.

   Sense nerves carry messages to the brain.

   a. _____

   _____

   _____

   b. _____

   _____

   _____

2. Motor nerves carry messages from the brain.

   The man hurt his motor nerves.

   The man was in an accident.

   a. _____

   _____

   _____

   _____

   b. _____

   _____

   _____

3. Jim was a baseball player.

   Jim spoke with his father.

   His father had strong biceps.

   a. _____

   _____

   _____

   b. _____

   _____

   _____

F Write a word that comes from **protect** or **consume** in each blank. Then write **verb, noun,** or **adjective** after each item.

1. _____ need to know more about products. _____

2. Some liquids give your stomach a _____ coating. _____

3. The fat cat _____ a lot of food. _____

4. The bone that _____ your brain is called the skull. _____

5. That burning candle is _____ oxygen. _____

G Fill in each blank.

1. _____

2. _____

3. _____

4. _____

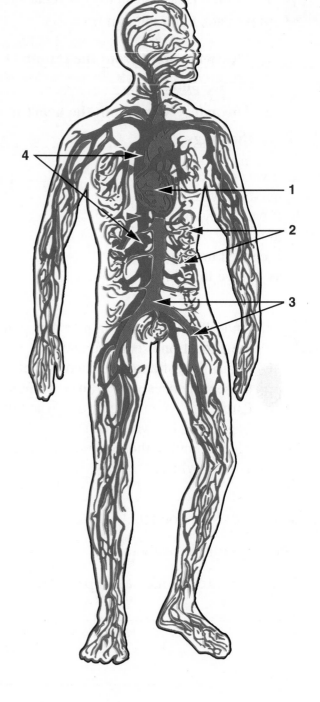

H Write **R** for each fact that is **relevant** to what happened.

Write **I** for each fact that is **irrelevant** to what happened.

Sam wants to modify his car.

1. His car leaks gas. _____

2. He paid for his car with cash. _____

3. Sam likes cars that are different. _____

4. He parks his car in the driveway. _____

I On your own lined paper, rewrite the paragraph by combining the sentences that are joined with an underline. If one of the sentences tells **why,** combine the sentences with **because.**

The brain is the most complex organ in the body. The brain belongs to the nervous system. The brain is very complicated. We do not fully understand the brain.   The brain has three parts. The three parts are the cerebrum, the cerebellum, and the medulla.   The cerebrum is larger than the medulla. The cerebellum is larger than the medulla.

J Write the instructions.

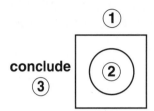

1. (what) _____

_____

2. (what and where) _____

_____

3. (what and where) _____

_____

_____

ERRORS	O	W	B	T

A Circle the subject and underline the predicate. Rewrite each sentence by moving part of the predicate.

1. You take in oxygen when you breathe.

_____

_____

2. They whistled as they worked.

_____

_____

3. Many crops are planted in the spring.

_____

_____

4. She reads books for the fun of it.

_____

_____

B Underline the common part. Combine the contradictory sentences with **but.** Combine the other sentences with **who** or **which.**

1. Pete went to school.

Pete wanted to stay home.

_____

_____

2. Pete went to school.

Pete had red hair.

_____

_____

3. A watch is very small.

A watch has more than two hundred parts.

_____

_____

_____

4. A watch is very small.

A watch tells time.

_____

_____

5. Fred likes to read.

Fred is a good student.

_____

_____

6. Fred likes to read.

Fred doesn't have any books.

_____

_____

_____

C Read the story and answer the questions. Circle the **W** if the question is answered by words in the story, and underline those words. Circle the **D** if the question is answered by a deduction.

Your brain has three parts: the cerebrum, the cerebellum, and the medulla. The cerebrum, which is by far the largest part, takes up the top half of your skull. It is the part that lets you think and feel. The cerebellum, which is under the back part of the cerebrum, regulates your muscular system. The medulla, which is the smallest part, is at the top of the spinal cord. It controls your digestive, circulatory, and respiratory systems.

1. Name the three parts of your brain.

_____

2. Which part is the smallest?

_____

3. Where is the cerebrum?

_____

_____

4. What does the cerebellum do?

_____

_____ **W**   **D**

5. Where is the cerebellum?

_____

_____ **W**   **D**

6. Which part do you use when you make a deduction?

_____ **W**   **D**

7. Which part regulates your heartbeat?

_____ **W**   **D**

D Write the instructions.

③ →   ↑
    │   │
    └─── ① ──── ②

1. (what) _____

_____

2. (what and where) _____

_____

_____

_____

3. (what and where) _____

_____

_____

_____

E Draw in the arrows. Shade in each tube that carries dark blood. Tell what gas each tube carries.

1. _____

2. _____

3. _____

4. _____

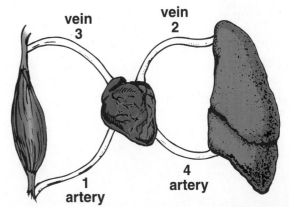

vein 3   vein 2

1 artery   4 artery

LESSON 22

F Write a word that comes from **predict** or **modify** in each blank. Then write **verb, noun,** or **adjective** after each item.

1. Your digestive system _____ food. _____

2. The weather _____ for today were right. _____

3. The heart does not _____ the blood. _____

4. Her remarks are always _____.
_____

5. Some products could be better with
_____ . _____

G Write **R** for each fact that is **relevant** to what happened. Write **I** for each fact that is **irrelevant** to what happened.

> **The woman's brain sent out this message: "Bend elbow."**

1. She had just stubbed her toe. _____

2. She was trying to catch a baseball. _____

3. She was bringing her hand to her eyes. _____

4. Her team was winning the game. _____

H This word means **a place where someone lives:** _____.

1. Cross out the words that tell what this word means.
2. Over the words you crossed out, print the word that means **a place where someone lives.**
3. At the end of the sentence, print the verb this word comes from.
4. Circle the adjectives.

I Make each statement mean the same thing as the statement in the box.

> **That factory regulates its production daily.**

1. That factory controls its production every day.

2. What that factory makes is criticized daily.

3. That factory controls its selection every day.

4. What that factory makes is regulated daily.

 A Underline the common part. Combine the contradictory sentences with **but.** Combine the other sentences with **who** or **which.**

1. These regulations are fair.

These regulations have always been ignored.

_____

_____

2. Ken modified his car.

His car still doesn't run.

_____

_____

3. Ken modified his car.

His car is red.

_____

_____

4. The barn was full of hay.

The barn had red doors.

_____

_____

5. Jennifer wanted to construct a house.

Jennifer didn't have any tools.

_____

_____

6. Jennifer wanted to construct a house.

Jennifer was six feet tall.

_____

_____

B Underline the contradiction. Circle the statement it contradicts. Tell **why** the underlined statement contradicts the circled statement.

The aorta is the biggest artery in your body. It is almost an inch wide. The blood in it carries oxygen to all parts of the body. * This blood looks almost black. The aorta is protected by your ribs. If it were ever cut, you probably would die.

_____

_____

Lester and Shirley were walking around town. They went to the park and to the zoo. Finally they came to a residential district. * They sat down on the curb. Lester said, "This place has almost no residences. It's not very exciting. Let's go back to the park."

_____

_____

_____

LESSON 23

C Read the story and answer the questions. Circle the **W** if the question is answered by words in the story, and underline those words. Circle the **D** if the question is answered by a deduction.

There are only two kinds of things you can obtain: things you need in order to live and things you don't need in order to live. Things you need are called needs. Things you don't need are called luxuries. Here are some needs: food, so you won't get hungry; clothes, so you won't get cold; a home, so you'll be protected from rain and snow. Here are some luxuries: a fancy food like lobster, a mink coat, a fifty-room vacation home on a lake. Here's a rule about luxuries: The richer you are, the more luxuries you can obtain. A rich person can have a mink coat; a poor person probably can't. A rich person can have a fifty-room vacation home; a poor person probably can't.

1. What do we call things you don't need?

_____

2. What do we call things you need?

_____

3. List three kinds of clothes that you need.

_____
_____
_____

4. List three kinds of clothes that you don't need.

_____
_____
_____

5. What's the rule about the richer you are?

_____
_____
_____ **W**   **D**

6. Mrs. Smith has a fur coat, an expensive sports car, and three homes.
Mrs. Jones has a cloth coat, a small car, and a one-room apartment.
Which person is probably richer?

_____ **W**   **D**

7. Mr. Coltrane earns $600 a month.
Mr. Thomas earns $600 a week.
Which person can get more luxuries?

_____ **W**   **D**

8. How do you know?

_____
_____ **W**   **D**

D Draw arrows that show which way messages move in each nerve.

sense   motor

——(brain)——

E Make each statement mean the same thing as the statement in the box.

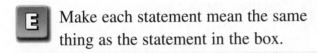

Cars consume gas and produce smoke.

1. Cars use up gas and consume smoke.

2. Cars make smoke and use up gas.

3. Cars consume smoke and make gas.

4. Cars, which produce smoke, use up gas.

F Draw in the arrows. Tell if each tube is a vein or an artery. Tell what gas each tube carries.

1. _____

2. _____

3. _____

4. _____

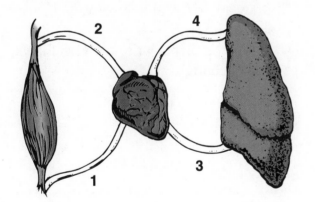

G Underline the nouns.
Draw a line **over** the adjectives.
Circle the verbs.

1. Sense nerves carry messages to the brain.

2. Consumers were complaining to the store manager.

3. The store consumes many paper products.

4. Motor nerves let people move.

H Fill in each blank.

1. _____

2. _____

3. _____

1. _____ nervous system

2 and 3. _____ nervous system

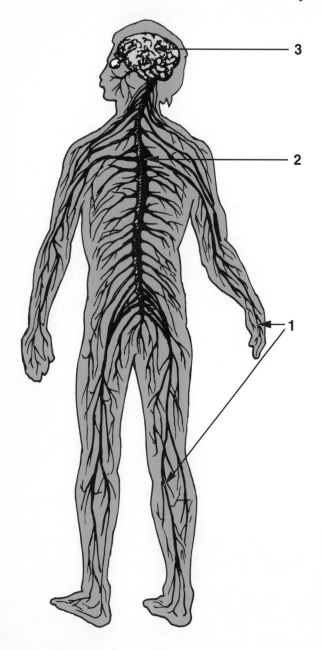

3

2

1

I Complete the analogies.

1. Tell what verb each word comes from.

   Conclusion is to _____

   as **conclusive** is to _____.

2. Tell what part of speech each word is.

   Conclusion is to _____

   as **conclusive** is to _____.

3. Tell what ending each word has.

   Conclusion is to _____

   as **conclusive** is to _____.

J Follow the directions.

1. Draw a line that slants up to the right.
2. Draw a line from the top of the slanted line that slants down to the right.
3. Draw a horizontal line between the two slanted lines.
4. Below the shape, write the verb that means **change.**

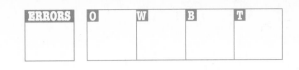

A Underline the common part. Combine the contradictory sentences with **but.** Combine the other sentences with **who** or **which.**

1. Linda has a broken femur.
   Linda can walk fast.

   _____

   _____

2. **Modify** is a verb.
   Modify means **change.**

   _____

   _____

3. John paid a lot for that radio.
   That radio doesn't work.

   _____

   _____

4. John paid a lot for that radio.
   That radio is green.

   _____

   _____

5. Sally was happy.
   Sally wore a red dress.

   _____

   _____

6. Sally was happy.
   Sally didn't smile.

   _____

   _____

B Rewrite the paragraph in four sentences on your own lined paper. If one of the sentences tells **why,** combine the sentences with **because.** If sentences seem contradictory, combine them with **but.**

Many animals are faster than people. People can run a hundred meters in ten seconds. A horse is faster. An antelope is faster. A good horse can run a hundred meters in six seconds. A hundred meters in six seconds is pretty fast. Horses seem very fast to us. Horses are much slower than some other animals.

C Underline the contradiction. Circle the statement it contradicts. Tell **why** the underlined statement contradicts the circled statement.

The doctor was giving a talk on the nervous system. He showed many slides of body parts. One slide showed the brain. * The doctor said, "This body part may not look like much, but it is very important. It is part of the peripheral nervous system. It controls everything your body does."

_____

_____

_____

Copyright © SRA/McGraw-Hill

Your brain regulates everything you do. It tells your heart when to beat. It tells your eyes how to read. * It tells your feet how to move. You couldn't do anything without it. It is controlled by your intestines.

_____

_____

 D Write a word that comes from **explain** in each blank. Then write **verb, noun,** or **adjective** after each item.

1. Last week, he _____ his reasons for leaving. _____

2. That _____ talk was very clear. _____

3. The teacher criticized my only _____. _____

4. He selected the best _____. _____

5. He needs someone to _____ math to him. _____

E Tell if each nerve is a **sense** nerve or a **motor** nerve. Draw an arrow to show which way the message moves.

1. "Hand feels cold."　　**2.** "Move hand."

3. "Turn head."　　**4.** "Throat is sore."

F Underline the nouns. Draw a line **over** the adjectives. Circle the verbs.

1. That motor nerve is carrying a message from the brain.

2. A teacher will explain those new rules.

3. The central nervous system is a complex body system.

4. Most new cars come with explanatory booklets.

G Tell **two** ways that the things compared are **not** the same.
Tell **one** way that the things compared **are** the same.

His voice was like a knife.

1. _____

_____

2. _____

_____

3. _____

_____

H Draw in the arrows. Shade in each tube that carries dark blood. Tell if each tube is a vein or an artery.

1. _____

2. _____

3. _____

4. _____

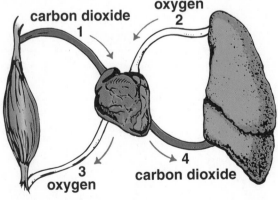

carbon dioxide 1 → oxygen 2 ← 3 oxygen → 4 carbon dioxide

I Use the rule to answer the questions.

The bigger the fire, the more carbon dioxide it produces.

1. What produces more carbon dioxide, a camp fire or a candle?

_____

2. Mary's camp fire produced a lot of carbon dioxide.
Tom's camp fire didn't produce much carbon dioxide.
a. Whose fire was bigger?

_____

b. How do you know?

_____

_____

3. Tom lit a match. Mary lit a pile of rags.
a. Which fire produced more carbon dioxide?

_____

b. How do you know?

_____

_____

J Read the story and answer the questions. Circle the **W** if the question is answered by words in the story, and underline those words. Circle the **D** if the question is answered by a deduction.

> **Here's a rule about needs and luxuries: Over time, some luxuries become needs. The first people on Earth didn't need much to live: raw meat, water, a cave. Later on, somebody discovered fire, and people started using it. They didn't really need fire, but they liked it. Now they could cook their food and warm their caves at night. Over time, they got so used to cooking food and keeping warm that they couldn't live without fire. Fire had become a need. The same thing happened with shoes, cups, plates, chairs, beds, and many other things. They started out as luxuries but ended up as needs.**

1. What are luxuries?

_____

_____

2. What's the rule about what happens over time?

_____

_____ **W**   **D**

3. Did people need fire at first?

_____

4. Did people need fire later?

_____

5. Name two new things that people could do with fire.

_____

_____ **W**   **D**

6. Here are some luxuries that became needs: shoes, cups, plates, and chairs. Name three more.

_____

7. Here are some luxuries that will never become needs: pet snakes, gold plates, and silver spoons. Name two more.

_____

K Follow the directions.

1. Draw a vertical line.
2. Draw a horizontal line that goes to the right from the top of the vertical line.
3. To the left of the vertical line, write **what burning things need.**
4. Above the horizontal line, write **what burning things produce.**

WORD LIST

Conclusion (n) *means* the end or something that is concluded.

Conclusive (a) *means* that something is true without any doubt.

Construction (n) *means* something that is constructed.

Consumable (a) *means* that something can be consumed.

Consume (v) *means* use up or eat.

Consumer (n) *means* something that consumes.

Modification (n) *means* a change.

Modify (v) *means* change.

Motor nerve (n) *means* a nerve that lets you move.

Obtain (v) *means* get.

Predictable (a) *means* that something is easy to predict.

Prediction (n) *means* a statement that predicts.

Sense nerve (n) *means* a nerve that lets you feel.

ERRORS	O	W	B	T

A Rewrite the paragraph in four sentences on your own lined paper. If one of the sentences tells **why,** combine the sentences with **because.** If sentences seem contradictory, combine them with **but.**

The cheetah is much faster than the horse. The cheetah has the strongest legs of any land animal. The cheetah lives in Africa. The cheetah lives in Asia. The cheetah doesn't start as fast as some animals. The cheetah can run a hundred meters in only three seconds. The cheetah eats only meat. The cheetah is a member of the cat family.

B Underline the common part. Combine the contradictory sentences with **but.** Combine the other sentences with **who** or **which.**

1. **Digestive** comes from the word **digest.**

   Digestive is an adjective.

   _____

   _____

   _____

2. Fran was tired.

   Fran didn't sleep.

   _____

   _____

3. Fran was tired.

   Fran had black hair.

   _____

   _____

4. Cod liver oil tastes terrible.

   Cod liver oil is good for you.

   _____

   _____

   _____

5. Some people eat a lot.

   Some people don't get fat.

   _____

   _____

6. **Digestive** comes from the word **digest.**

   Digest is a verb.

   _____

   _____

   _____

C Underline the contradiction. Circle the statement it contradicts. Tell **why** the underlined statement contradicts the circled statement.

The vena cava is the biggest vein in your body. It is very close to your heart. It carries blood from all the muscle cells to the heart. * The vena cava carries a lot of oxygen. It looks almost black. Every bit of blood passes through the vena cava at some time.

_____

_____

Linda and Jim went to a film. The film concluded with a shot of people kissing. Jim did not like the film. * He was happy when the film was over. He said, "I hate films that begin with kissing." Linda thought that Jim was being silly.

_____

_____

D Tell if each nerve is a **sense** nerve or a **motor** nerve. Draw an arrow to show which way the message moves.

1. "Knee hurts."   **2.** "Sneeze."

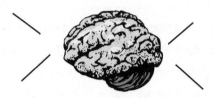

3. "Bend knee."   **4.** "Nose itches."

E Circle the subject and underline the predicate. Rewrite the sentence by moving the predicate.

1. Don was happy because he passed the test.

_____

_____

2. That strong old woman will grin if she wins.

_____

_____

3. You can't go to Spain without a passport.

_____

_____

4. She wore her mittens because it was snowing.

_____

_____

F Read the story and answer the questions.
Circle the **W** if the question is answered by words in the story, and underline those words.
Circle the **D** if the question is answered by a deduction.

> **Here's a rule about ads: Some ads try to make luxuries a need. Let's say a woman sells watches, which are a luxury. She has to sell a lot of watches to get rich. So, she puts an ad on TV that says "Everybody needs a watch. It tells you the time all day long. You'll never be late to class. You'll never be late to work. A watch feels good on your wrist, and it doesn't cost much." Some people who see the ad will think that they really do need a watch, and they will buy one. If lots of people feel the same way, the woman will get rich. Remember, her ad tried to make a luxury a need.**

1. What's the rule about some ads?

_____

_____

2. Why does the woman have to sell a lot of watches?

_____ **W**   **D**

3. What will some people who see the ad think?

_____

_____ **W**   **D**

4. What will they do next?

_____ **W**   **D**

5. Which luxury do you think is easier to make into a need: a microwave oven or a toy train?

_____ **W**   **D**

6. "This balloon is only for the very rich. It takes a long time to fill with air, and you can only use it in the summer."
Does this ad try to make a luxury a need?

_____

7. Do you think the ad will sell many balloons?

_____

8. Why?

_____

_____

G Write the instructions.

① _____

explanatory
③
② _____

1. (what) _____

_____

2. (what and where) _____

_____

_____

3. (what and where) _____

_____

_____

[H] Write a word that comes from **explain** in each blank. Then write **verb, noun,** or **adjective** after each item.

1. She put _____ notes at the

end of her paper. _____

2. The traffic cop asked her for an

_____. _____

3. Can you _____ this

problem? _____

4. I will _____ these critical

remarks. _____

5. His _____ was very

conclusive. _____

ERRORS | O | W | B | T

A Use the facts to fill out the form.

> **Facts: Your name is Jeff Miller. You were born on May 26, 1976. You are applying for a job at the post office. Your last job was driving a truck for the Ace Trucking Company. You worked there for two years, but had to quit when you got scarlet fever. Your address is 16 Ward Avenue, Springfield, Ohio.**

Instructions:

1. Name (last name first):

_____

2. Date of birth: _____

3. Today's date: _____

4. Address: _____

_____

5. Whom did you last work for? _____

_____

6. For how long? _____

7. Reasons for leaving: _____

_____

B Underline the contradiction. Circle the statement it contradicts. Tell **why** the underlined statement contradicts the circled statement.

> Kit wrote a sentence. It was very long. It had six adjectives. * It was about her father. It had only a predicate. It was a pretty good sentence.

_____

_____

_____

> The man came home on a cold winter night. He started a fire in his fireplace, but his chimney was clogged. He took off his coat and hat. * Pretty soon, he noticed that something was wrong. His house was beginning to fill up with oxygen. He had to open the window, which let the cold air in. The man became very mad.

_____

_____

C Write the instructions.

1. (what and where) _____

_____

2. (what and where) _____

_____

_____

3. (what and where) _____

_____

_____

D Write the middle part of each deduction.

1. Blood that is red carries oxygen.

_____

_____

So, blood in the pulmonary vein carries oxygen.

2. Some bones do not support the body.

_____

_____

So, maybe the scapula does not support the body.

3. Fred has every kind of artery.

_____

_____

So, Fred has an aorta.

E Tell which fact each statement relates to. Make each contradiction true.

| 1. **People have arteries in their cheeks.** |
| 2. **People have sense nerves in their cheeks.** |

a. They carry dark blood. _____

b. They carry messages from the brain. _____

c. They carry oxygen. _____

d. They carry messages like: "Move cheek." _____

LESSON 26

F Circle the subject and underline the predicate. Rewrite the sentence by moving part of the predicate.

1. Her bones get stronger as she grows older.

_____

_____

2. Sally sees better when she wears her glasses.

_____

_____

3. He turned the dial to regulate the heat.

_____

_____

4. Those animals let out carbon dioxide when they breathe.

_____

_____

_____

G Fill in each blank.

1. _____

2. _____

3. _____

4. _____

5. _____

6. _____

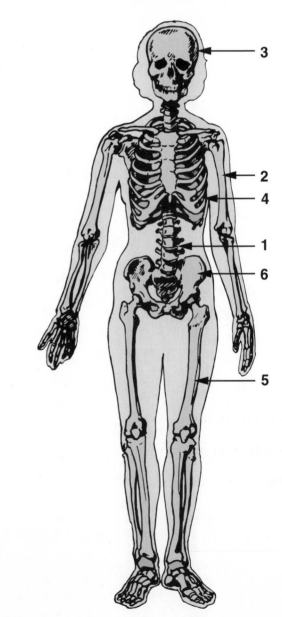

H Underline the common part. Circle the word that combines the sentences correctly. Combine the sentences with that word.

1. The femur is the upper leg bone.

The quadriceps covers part of the femur.

which   and   but

_____

_____

_____

2. That car has red stripes.

This wagon has red stripes.

which   and   because

_____

_____

3. A thick book was on the table.

Ten pens were on the table.

and   but   because

_____

_____

4. Whales are not fish.

Whales live in the water.

who   but   because

_____

_____

5. His wide-brimmed hat is white.

Her new long dress is white.

and   but   because

_____

_____

_____

I Tell if each nerve is a **sense** nerve or a **motor** nerve. Draw an arrow to show which way the message moves.

1. "Finger hurts."   **2.** "Bend leg."

3. "Scratch arm."   **4.** "Strong smell."

ERRORS | O | W | B | T

A Write the instructions.

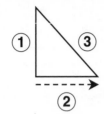

1. (what) _____

_____

2. (what and where) _____

_____

_____

_____

3. (what and where) _____

_____

_____

B Underline the contradiction.
Circle the statement it contradicts.
Tell **why** the underlined statement
contradicts the circled statement.

Sam hurt his arm. So he went to see a
doctor. The doctor examined Sam. The
doctor took some X rays and he gave Sam
some drugs that would reduce the pain.
Then the doctor told Sam, "You have a
sore femur. It should feel better in a few
days."

_____

_____

C Use the facts to fill out the form.

**Facts: You are applying for a
driver's license. You live at 1605
Willow Boulevard, Bellingham,
Washington. Your phone number is
725-1020. You have never had a
driver's license before. You took a
driver training class in high school.
You wear glasses. Your name is
Cristina Lopez.**

Instructions:

1. Phone number: _____

2. Have you had any driver training? _____

3. If so, where? _____

4. Full address: _____

_____

5. Last name: _____

6. Sex: _____

7. Do you wear glasses? _____

D Make up a simile for each item.

1. A man had bright eyes.

_____

_____

2. A woman was smart.

_____

E Tell if each nerve is a **sense** nerve or a **motor** nerve. Draw an arrow to show which way the message moves.

1. "Curl toes."   2. "Food smells good."

3. "Lie down."   4. "Feel tired."

F Underline the common part. Circle the word that combines the sentences correctly. Combine the sentences with that word.

1. John studied hard.

   John did not pass the test.

   because   but   which

   _____

   _____

2. The mouth belongs to the digestive system.

   The esophagus belongs to the digestive system.

   but   and   which

   _____

   _____

   _____

3. His mother is explaining the rules.

   His father is explaining the rules.

   and   but   which

   _____

   _____

4. This stream was moving fast.

   That river was moving fast.

   because   who   and

   _____

   _____

5. Oregon is covered with trees.

   Oregon has many lumber mills.

   who   but   because

   _____

   _____

   _____

G Write the conclusion of each deduction.

1. Some blood vessels go to the heart.
Venules are blood vessels.

_____

_____

2. Some bones support your body.
The scapula is a bone.

_____

_____

3. Blood that is almost black carries carbon dioxide.
Blood in the arm veins is almost black.

_____

_____

_____

H Write a word that comes from **predict** or **digest** in each blank. Then write **verb, noun,** or **adjective** after each item.

1. Andy is _____ the winner of

the game. _____

2. Her _____ system makes

strange sounds. _____

3. She drank milk to help her _____.

_____

4. Things that are _____ are

dull. _____

5. The fortune-teller loved to make

_____. _____

I Circle the subject and underline the predicate. Rewrite the sentence by moving part of the predicate.

1. This big green truck is fast when it works.

_____

_____

2. Your body needs all six nutrients to stay

healthy.

_____

_____

_____

3. Pete is working longer to increase his

production.

_____

_____

4. All cups are containers because they can hold

things.

_____

_____

J Fill in each blank.

1. _____

2. _____

3. _____

4. _____

5. _____

6. _____

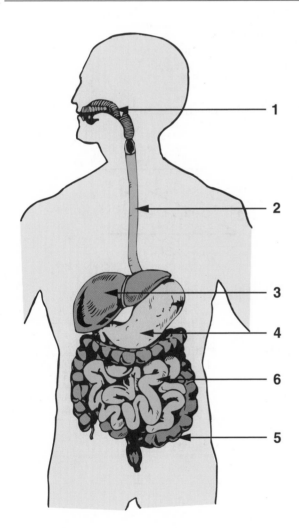

K Write what each analogy tells.

> What each kind of nerve lets you do
>
> What body system each nerve belongs to
>
> What each nerve carries
>
> Which direction messages move in each kind of nerve

1. **Sense nerves** are to **to the brain** as **motor nerves** are to **from the brain.**

_____

_____

2. **Sense nerves** are to **feeling** as **motor nerves** are to **moving**.

_____

_____

3. **Sense nerves** are to the **nervous system** as **motor nerves** are to the **nervous system**.

_____

_____

ERRORS	O	W	B	T

A Make up a simile for each item.

1. A man ran fast.

_____

_____

2. A woman's arms were thin.

_____

_____

B Label each nerve.
Write a message for each nerve.

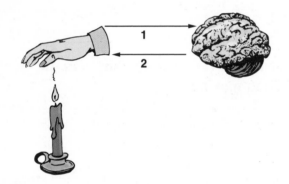

1. _____

2. _____

C Write **R** for each fact that is **relevant** to what happened. Write **I** for each fact that is **irrelevant** to what happened.

The man's brain sent out this message: "Biceps hurts."

1. The man was wearing tall boots. _____

2. The man's upper arm had just been stung by a bee. _____

3. The man had hit his arm to kill the bee. _____

4. The man was six feet tall. _____

D Write the instructions.

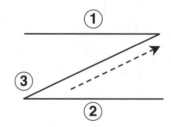

1. (what) _____

_____

2. (what and where) _____

_____

_____

3. (what and where) _____

_____

_____

_____

E Complete the analogies.

1. Tell what each kind of nerve lets you do.
   Sense nerves are to letting you

   _____

   as motor nerves are to letting you

   _____

2. Tell what body system each nerve belongs to.
   Sense nerves are to the

   _____ system

   as motor nerves are to the

   _____ system.

3. Tell which direction each kind of nerve
   message moves in.
   Sense nerves are to

   _____ the brain

   as motor nerves are to

   _____ the brain.

F Underline the contradiction. Circle the
   statement it contradicts. Tell **why** the
   underlined statement contradicts the
   circled statement.

One day, Ellen fell down the stairs.
She hurt one of the nerves in her spinal
cord. She broke three ribs. * The doctor
said that Ellen would have to stay in bed
for a long time. He told her that she had
hurt a nerve in her peripheral nervous
system. He also told her that she had
broken a part of her skeletal system.

_____

_____

G Fill in each blank with the word that has
   the same meaning as the word or words
   under the blank.

1. We stayed until the _____ of
                                    (end)
   the concert.

2. Dentists _____ many teeth
                  (look at)
   every day.

3. Some things are very easy to

   _____.
     (find fault with)

4. People cannot _____ storms.
                        (make)

5. To save gas, this car must be _____.
                                    (changed)

H Underline the common part. Circle the word that combines the sentences correctly. Combine the sentences with that word.

1. Ohio is in the Midwest.

Ohio borders Lake Erie.

which   because   who

_____

_____

2. A body has many parts.

An engine has many parts.

because   and   who

_____

_____

3. Mary has big biceps.

Mary can't lift heavy things.

because   which   but

_____

_____

_____

4. Plants are living things.

Plants produce oxygen.

which   but   who

_____

_____

5. His tall uncle runs every morning.

His slim aunt runs every morning.

and   who   but

_____

_____

I Draw in the arrows. Shade in each tube that carries dark blood. Tell what gas each tube carries.

1. _____

2. _____

3. _____

4. _____

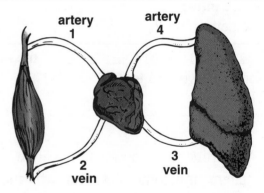

artery 1   artery 4

2 vein   3 vein

J Read the story and answer the questions. Circle the **W** if the question is answered by words in the story, and underline those words. Circle the **D** if the question is answered by a deduction.

Cars as we know them were first made around 1900. They cost a lot, and only rich people could buy them. A man named Henry Ford thought that he could make a lot of money if he produced cheap cars that anybody could buy. He started the Ford Motor Company in 1903 and sold his first cars for $850, which was a lot cheaper than any other car. But Ford wanted to make his cars even cheaper. He followed one rule: The lower the price, the bigger the sales. Each year more people bought them. By 1914, a Ford cost only $500, and one half of all cars made were Fords.

1. About how many years ago were the first cars made?

_____

_____ **W**   **D**

2. How did Henry Ford think he could make a lot of money?

_____

_____ **W**   **D**

3. How much cheaper was a 1914 Ford than a 1903 Ford?

_____ **W**   **D**

4. What rule did Ford follow?

_____

_____ **W**   **D**

5. Car A and Car B are very much alike. Car A costs $3,000. Car B costs $5,000. Which car will have bigger sales?

_____

6. How do you know?

_____

_____

7. How much do you think a Ford costs now?

_____

_____

A Combine the sentences with **particularly.**

1. Your blood moves fast.
Your blood moves fastest when you run.

_____

_____

2. John reads books.
John reads the most books when he is at home.

_____

_____

3. The sun is bright.
The sun is brightest in the summer.

_____

_____

4. They have a lot of fun.
They have the most fun when they play darts.

_____

_____

_____

B Label each nerve.
Write a message for each nerve.

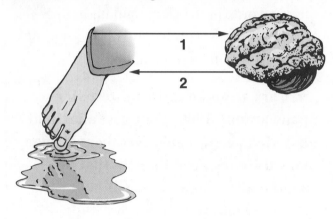

1. _____

2. _____

C Write a word that comes from **manufacture** in each blank. Then write **verb, noun,** or **adjective** after each item.

1. That car _____ makes a lot of money. _____

2. He is _____ buttons for coats. _____

3. Some _____ products fall apart quickly. _____

4. That _____ will modify his line of cars. _____

5. That factory _____ toys every day. _____

D Read the story and answer the questions. Circle the **W** if the question is answered by words in the story, and underline those words. Circle the **D** if the question is answered by a deduction.

> **Henry Ford made cars a need. Before 1900, cars were a luxury. People didn't need them to get places because they walked or took a train. But when people started buying Fords, other people would say, "If you own a Ford, you don't have to walk or take a train. I like that." And then they would buy Fords. Pretty soon, lots and lots of people had Fords. Cities had to construct new streets for all the cars. People moved from apartments in the city to houses in the suburbs. It took just as long to drive your car from your suburban house to the store as it did to walk from your city apartment to the store. By 1920, things had changed so much that many people really needed a car to live. What had started out as a luxury was now a need.**

1. What did Henry Ford make cars?

_____ **W**   **D**

2. Why were cars a luxury before Ford?

_____

_____ **W**   **D**

3. How did people think they could stop having to walk everywhere?

_____

4. Where did people move to? _____

_____ **W**   **D**

5. Did it take any longer to get to the store if you lived in the suburbs and had a car?

_____

6. About how long did it take to make cars a need?

_____ **W**   **D**

7. Name two other luxuries that have been made needs since the car.

_____

E Underline the nouns. Draw a line **over** the adjectives. Circle the verbs.

1. Poets write many similes.

2. Her boss runs six miles every day.

3. Bicycles are manufactured products.

4. That plant manufactured bicycles and motorcycles.

F Draw in the arrows. Tell if each tube is a **vein** or an **artery.** Tell what gas each tube carries.

1. _____

2. _____

3. _____

4. _____

LESSON 29

G Write the middle part of each deduction.

1. Feelings go to the brain.

_____

So, pain goes to the brain.

2. Commands travel on motor nerves.

_____

So, "Nod head" travels on a motor nerve.

3. Some animals have no bones.

_____

So, maybe a snail has no bones.

_____
The digestive system changes food

into fuel.
_____

1. Circle the adjectives.
2. Cross out the nouns.
3. Underline the words that tell what the digestive system does.
4. Underline the words that tell what body system the large intestine is in.

I Underline the contradiction. Circle the statement it contradicts. Tell why the underlined statement contradicts the circled statement.

The pulmonary vein is the only vein in the body that carries oxygen. It is also one of the biggest veins in the body. * It goes from the lungs to the heart. It looks black. It is part of the circulatory system.

_____

_____

J Tell **two** ways that the things compared are **not** the same.
Tell **one** way that the things compared **are** the same.

_____
The coach talked like a machine

gun.
_____

1. _____

_____

2. _____

_____

3. _____

_____

Follow the directions.

1. Draw a horizontal line.
2. Draw another horizontal line below the first line.
3. Draw a line that slants from the right end of the top line to the left end of the bottom line.
4. To the right of the slanted line, write the verb that means **end.**

WORD LIST

Arteries (n) *means* the tubes that carry blood away from the heart.

Capillaries (n) *means* the very small tubes that connect the arteries and veins.

Circulatory system (n) *means* the body system that moves blood around the body.

Consume (v) *means* use up or eat.

Critical (a) *means* that something criticizes.

Digestion (n) *means* the act of digesting.

Explain (v) *means* make something easier to understand.

Explanation (n) *means* something that explains.

Explanatory (a) *means* that something explains.

Heart (n) *means* the pump that moves the blood.

Productive (a) *means* that something produces a lot of things.

Protect (v) *means* guard.

Simile (n) *means* a statement that tells how things are the same.

Veins (n) *means* the tubes that carry blood back to the heart.

ERRORS	O	W	B	T

A   Combine the sentences with **particularly.**

1. He cooks good food.
He cooks the best food when people come for dinner.

_____

_____

_____

2. Your bones are strong.
Your bones are strongest if you drink lots of milk.

_____

_____

_____

3. She gets angry.
She gets the angriest when people criticize her.

_____

_____

4. That dog is noisy.
That dog is the noisiest when it is outside.

_____

_____

B   Tell **two** ways that the things compared are **not** the same.
Tell **one** way that the things compared **are** the same.

His hands were like spider legs.

1. _____

_____

2. _____

_____

3. _____

_____

C   Draw in the arrows. Shade in each tube that carries dark blood. Tell what gas each tube carries.

1. _____

2. _____

3. _____

4. _____

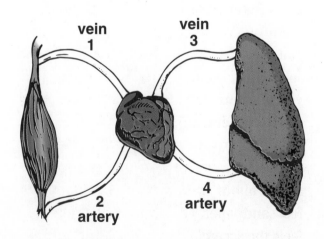

D Underline the nouns. Draw a line **over** the adjectives. Circle the verbs.

1. The woman's sense nerves let her feel.

2. That store sells many different manufactured goods.

3. A factory was manufacturing tires.

4. People think and feel with their brains.

E Read the story and answer the questions. Circle the **W** if the question is answered by words in the story, and underline those words. Circle the **D** if the question is answered by a deduction.

Your cerebrum, which is the most important part of your brain, is divided into two parts. The right side is called the right hemisphere and the left side is called the left hemisphere. In most people, the right hemisphere feels and the left hemisphere thinks. When you see, hear, smell, or feel, you use your right hemisphere. When you think about what you see, hear, smell, or feel, you use your left hemisphere. When you solve a problem or make a deduction, you use your left hemisphere. You often use both hemispheres at the same time. When you read, your right hemisphere sees the words and your left hemisphere thinks about what they mean. When you feel sandpaper, your right hemisphere feels the scratchiness and your left hemisphere concludes that it is sandpaper.

1. What are the two parts of the cerebrum?

_____

_____

2. What does the right hemisphere do?

_____ **W**   **D**

3. What does the left hemisphere do?

_____ **W**   **D**

4. Tell which hemisphere you would use to do the following things:

   a. Think about a story _____

   b. Look at something _____

   c. Smell something _____

   d. Solve a math problem _____

5. Tell if you use your right hemisphere or both hemispheres:

   a. Hearing a question _____

   b. Hearing a question and answering it _____

   c. Smelling something _____

   d. Smelling something and thinking it is a hamburger _____

LESSON 30

F Label each nerve.
Write a message for each nerve.

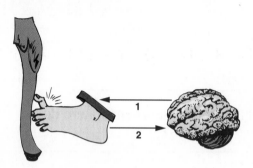

1. _____

2. _____

G Write a word that comes from **manufacture** in each blank. Then write **verb, noun,** or **adjective** after each item.

1. Doctors cannot _____ a

   human brain. _____

2. Pat predicts that the _____

   product will be popular. _____

3. Big companies _____ TVs

   every day. _____

4. Some companies _____

   chairs. _____

5. That factory has _____ a

   new line of dresses. _____

H Follow the directions.

1. Draw a horizontal line.

2. Draw a line that slants up to the right from the right end of the horizontal line.

3. At the left end of the horizontal line, draw an arrow that points up.

4. Draw the muscle that will move the horizontal line in the direction of the arrow.

```
┌─────────────────────────┐
│                         │
│                         │
│                         │
│                         │
└─────────────────────────┘
```

I Underline the contradiction. Circle the statement it contradicts. Tell **why** the underlined statement contradicts the circled statement.

John was wandering around a dark room. He stubbed his toe on a chair leg. The message "Toe hurts" went to his brain. * John jumped up and down. The message went on a motor nerve. John was in great pain for a long time. Finally, he stopped jumping up and down.

_____

_____

A Combine the sentences with **particularly.**

1. Cheetahs are fast.
   Cheetahs are fastest when they are hunting.

   _____

   _____

2. Mary writes well.
   Mary writes the best when she is alone.

   _____

   _____

3. Pete talks a lot.
   Pete talks the most at parties.

   _____

   _____

4. Muscles get sore.
   Muscles get sorest after you work hard.

   _____

   _____

B Make up a simile for each item.

1. A man's hands were smooth.

   _____

   _____

2. A woman's shirt had a lot of holes.

   _____

   _____

C Rewrite the paragraph in four sentences on your own lined paper. If one of the sentences tells **why,** combine the sentences with **because.** If sentences seem contradictory, combine them with **but.**

Fred wanted to read a book. Fred turned on the light. The book had a coffee stain on the first page. Fred could not read the book. Fred drank coffee. Fred had not made the stain. He went to see his mother. His mother was in the next room.

D Write the instructions.

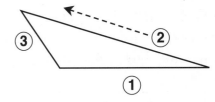

1. (what) _____

   _____

2. (what and where) _____

   _____

   _____

3. (what and where) _____

   _____

LESSON 31

E Label each nerve.
Write a message for each nerve.

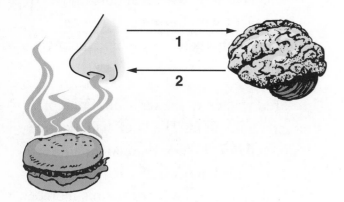

1. _____

2. _____

F Circle the subject and underline the predicate. Rewrite each sentence by moving part of the predicate.

1. The man was tired by noon.

_____

_____

2. The cat came home after three o'clock.

_____

_____

3. She wore a coat because it was very cold.

_____

_____

4. He won the race by running the fastest.

_____

_____

G Underline the contradiction. Circle the statement it contradicts. Tell **why** the underlined statement contradicts the circled statement.

From the outside, your upper arm looks pretty simple. But inside, many complex things are happening. Arteries are carrying blood to your biceps. Sense nerves are sending feelings to the brain. * The nerves carry little bits of electricity. The arteries carry carbon dioxide. All this is going on, but you never have to think about it.

_____

_____

H Make each statement mean the same thing as the statement in the box.

Her explanatory talk was hard to understand.

1. Her talk that explained was hard to understand.

2. It was easy to understand her explanatory talk.

3. It was hard to understand her talk that explained.

4. Her talk, which was explanatory, was difficult to understand.

I Fill in each blank.

1. _____

2. _____

3. _____

1 and 3. _____ nervous system

2. _____ nervous system

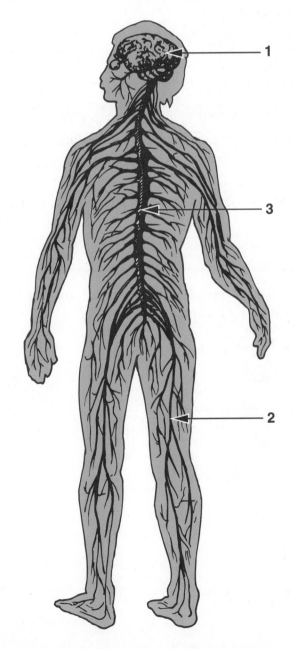

J Write a word that comes from **produce** or **explain** in each blank. Then write **verb, noun,** or **adjective** after each item.

1. _____ may be increased by combining some jobs. _____

2. An _____ would help me understand. _____

3. Most businesses try to be more _____. _____

4. She _____ herself very well. _____

5. Some digestive organs _____ chemicals. _____

K Read the story and answer the questions. Circle the **W** if the question is answered by words in the story, and underline those words.

Circle the **D** if the question is answered by a deduction.

> **When you walk, your body is doing thousands of things every minute. Your heart is beating; your leg muscles are pulling; your blood is moving. If your cerebrum had to think about doing all these things, it wouldn't have much time for anything else. This is why you have the cerebellum and the medulla. They regulate all the body parts you never think about. The cerebellum controls the muscular system. The medulla controls the digestive, circulatory, and respiratory systems.**

1. When you walk, your heart is beating, your leg muscles are pulling, and your blood is moving. Name three other things that your body is doing.

   _____

   _____

   _____

2. Why doesn't your cerebrum think about all those things?

   _____

   _____

   _____ **W**   **D**

3. Which system does the cerebellum regulate?

   _____ **W**   **D**

4. Which systems does the medulla regulate?

   _____

   _____ **W**   **D**

5. Tell which part of the brain you use for the following things:

   a. bending an arm   _____

   b. reading   _____

   c. listening to the   _____
      radio

   d. running   _____

   e. pumping blood   _____

A Use the facts to fill out the form.

> **Facts: Your name is Mack Johnson.**
> **You are applying for a bank loan.**
> **You have worked for the Maxwell**
> **Pen Company for five years. You**
> **make $3000 a month. You own a**
> **1992 compact car. You are married**
> **and have two children. You had to**
> **take out a loan to pay for the car.**
> **You want this bank loan to construct**
> **a house.**

Instructions:
a. Print your full name, last name first, on line 5.
b. Enter the name of the company you work for on line 2.
c. On line 3, describe the type of car you drive.
d. State your monthly income on line 1.
e. Enter the total number of people in your family on line 4.
f. On line 6, tell why you want the loan.
g. On line 7, write the second sentence above that gives information you didn't use in filling out the form.

1. _____

2. _____

3. _____

4. _____

5. _____

6. _____

7. _____

_____

_____

B Make up a simile for each item.

1. The town was busy.

_____

_____

2. She talked in a sweet way.

_____

_____

C Combine the sentences with **particularly.**

1. Your digestive system works hard.
Your digestive system works hardest after you eat.

_____

_____

_____

2. Tony swims fast.
Tony swims fastest in races.

_____

_____

3. Claire is a productive person.
Claire is the most productive when she works alone.

_____

_____

4. Stars look bright.
Stars look brightest outside the city.

_____

_____

D Underline the contradiction. Circle the statement it contradicts. Tell **why** the underlined statement contradicts the circled statement.

If you are losing a foot race, your brain sends out the message "Move faster" to your legs. Whether or not your legs will move faster depends on many things. All your body systems must work together. * The heart must pump more blood to the gastrocnemius and the quadriceps. The lungs must take in more air. The message must go over a sense nerve.

_____

_____

E Write a word that comes from **select** or **regulate** in each blank. Then write **verb, noun,** or **adjective** after each item.

1. Many people don't like to _____

a new car. _____

2. New stop signs will _____

the traffic. _____

3. The boss was very _____ in

hiring new people. _____

4. They did not _____ enough

fruit for lunch. _____

5. The army has _____ about

everything. _____

F Draw in the arrows. Shade in each tube that carries dark blood. Tell what gas each tube carries.

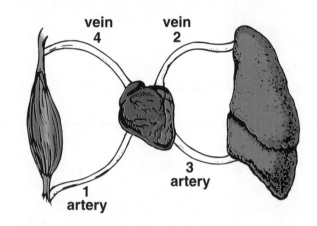

1. _____

2. _____

3. _____

4. _____

G Circle the subject and underline the predicate. Rewrite each sentence by moving part of the predicate.

1. The halls are white upstairs.

   _____

   _____

2. She goes to the store every morning.

   _____

   _____

3. They rolled down the hill for the fun of it.

   _____

   _____

4. He went to the beach to swim.

   _____

   _____

H Write the instructions.

1. (what and where) _____

   _____

2. (what and where) _____

   _____

   _____

3. (what and where) _____

   _____

I Rewrite the paragraph in four sentences on your own lined paper. If one of the sentences tells **why,** combine the sentences with **because.** If sentences seem contradictory, combine them with **but.**

   Cape Horn is on Horn Island. Horn Island is below the southern tip of South America. Sailors are afraid of sailing around the cape. The cape has very dangerous waves. The waves get very big. The waves get biggest in the winter. The cape is near the South Pole. The cape gets very cold.

ERRORS | O | W | B | T

A

Underline the contradiction. Circle the statement it contradicts. Tell **why** the underlined statement contradicts the circled statement. Make the underlined statement true.

Ted was sick, so he went to see a doctor. The doctor shot some medicine into one of Ted's veins. The doctor said, "This medicine will make you well again. * It will kill the germs in your circulatory system that are making you sick. Right now, the medicine is going away from your heart. You should be feeling better by tomorrow."

_____

_____

B

Make up a simile for each item.

1. The man's voice was very sharp.

_____

_____

2. The woman talked very fast.

_____

_____

C

Use the facts to fill out the form.

Facts: Your name is Alice Brown. You are applying for a credit card at the Paris Department Store. You are making payments of $150 a month on your car. You have lived at 144 Stone Avenue, Atlanta, Georgia, for one year. You have worked as a secretary for Jones Manufacturing for three years. You make $2000 a month, and you spend about $1700 a month.

Instructions:

1. Last name: _____

2. Street address: _____

_____

3. Monthly income: _____

4. Place of work: _____

_____

5. Monthly expenses: _____

6. Do you own or are you making payments on

a car? _____

7. Subtract expenses from income and write the number on line 1.

D Tell if each nerve is a **sense** nerve or a **motor** nerve. Draw an arrow to show which way the message moves.

1. "Head hurts."   **2.** "Toes are cold."

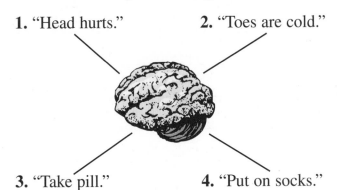

3. "Take pill."   **4.** "Put on socks."

E Circle the word that combines the sentences correctly. Combine the sentences with that word.

1. Gwenn was older than Jim.
Patrick was older than Jim.
but   which   and

_____

_____

2. John is very sick.
John won't go to the doctor.
particularly   which   but

_____

_____

3. Milk contains vitamin D.
Cheese contains vitamin D.
particularly   because   and

_____

_____

4. That stream moves fast.
That stream moves fastest down Rose Hill.
and   particularly   who

_____

_____

_____

5. Smokers have poor circulation.
Smokers don't breathe well.
and   which   but

_____

_____

_____

F Tell what gas each tube carries. Shade in each tube that carries dark blood. Tell if each tube is a **vein** or an **artery**.

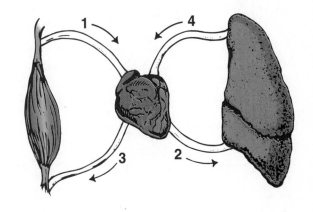

1. _____

2. _____

3. _____

4. _____

G Write the middle part of each deduction.

1. Ruth has had some diseases.

   _____

   So, maybe Ruth has had the mumps.

2. Commands come from the brain.

   _____

   So, "Move leg" comes from the brain.

3. Some plants cannot be eaten.

   _____

   So, maybe ferns cannot be eaten.

H Write the instructions.

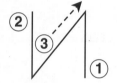

1. (what) _____

   _____

2. (what and where) _____

   _____

   _____

3. (what and where) _____

   _____

   _____

   _____

I Fill in each blank.

1. _____

2. _____

3. _____

4. _____

5. _____

6. _____

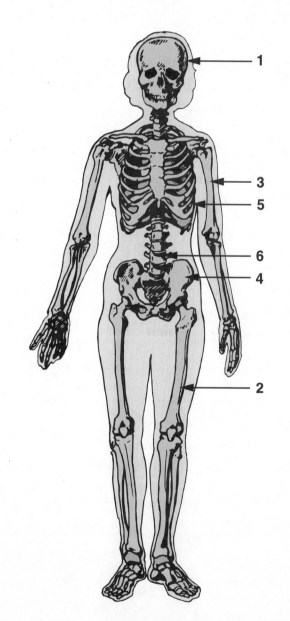

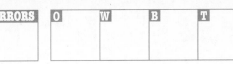
A Underline the contradiction. Circle the statement it contradicts. Tell **why** the underlined statement contradicts the circled statement. Make the underlined statement true.

A woman was in a bad car accident, and she blacked out. When she came to, she couldn't feel anything in her left hand. She was in a hospital bed. * A doctor told her that she was going to be operated on. She had cut a motor nerve. The woman felt lucky to be alive.

_____

_____

B Write a word that comes from **participate** in each blank. Then write **verb, noun,** or **adjective** after each item.

1. Last year he _____ in the

   production. _____

2. Volleyball is a _____ sport.

   _____

3. Teachers regulate classroom

   _____ . _____

4. He hates to _____ in plays.

   _____

5. They asked for Ann's _____

   in the game. _____

C Write the instructions.

③ vein   ② artery

①

1. _____

   _____

2. _____

   _____

   _____

3. _____

   _____

   _____

D   Make up a simile for each item.

1. She swims very well.

_____

2. The man had a bald head.

_____

_____

E   Read the story and answer the questions.
Circle the **W** if the question is answered
by words in the story, and underline
those words.
Circle the **D** if the question is answered
by a deduction.

Here's a rule about demand and
supply: When the demand is greater
than the supply, prices go up. Mr. Jones
runs the only dairy farm near Mudville.
In January, his cows produce just as
much milk as Mudville needs. Mr. Jones
makes $1000 from milk sales that month.
In February, his cows produce a lot less
milk than Mudville needs. If Mr. Jones
sells the milk at the old price, he won't
make $1000 because he doesn't have as
much milk to sell. But Mr. Jones wants to
make $1000, so he raises his prices.
Mudville's demand for milk is much
greater than Mr. Jones's supply, and he
has no trouble selling his milk at the
higher price. People in Mudville may not
like the higher price, but they know that
they need milk and that Mr. Jones's farm
is the only place where they can get milk.

1. What's the rule about demand and supply?

_____

_____

_____

2. Was the demand greater than the supply in January?

_____   **W**   **D**

3. Which was greater in February, the demand or the supply?

_____   **W**   **D**

4. If Mr. Jones sells his milk at the old price, why won't he make $1000?

_____

_____   **W**   **D**

5. Why did he raise his prices?

_____

_____

6. Why didn't he have any trouble selling the milk at the higher price?

_____

_____

_____   **W**   **D**

7. Give two reasons why the people of Mudville pay the higher price, even though they don't like it.

1. _____

_____

2. _____

_____

_____

8. Did the demand become greater than the supply because the supply went down or because the demand went up?

_____

_____ **W**   **D**

F Fill in each blank.

1. _____

2. _____

3. _____

4. _____

5. _____

6. _____

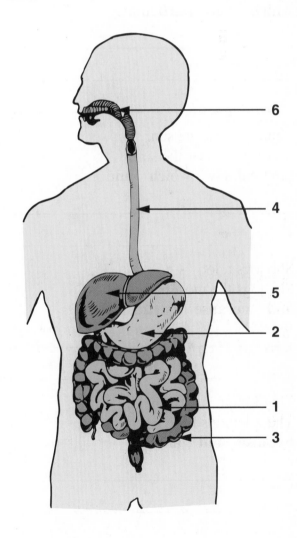

G Circle the word that combines the sentences correctly. Combine the sentences with that word.

1. Trees need carbon dioxide.
Bushes need carbon dioxide.
who   particularly   and

_____

_____

2. Animals are living things.
Animals produce carbon dioxide.
which   but   particularly

_____

_____

3. Venus is near the sun.
Mercury is near the sun.
particularly   which   and

_____

_____

4. She jogs a lot.
She jogs the most before races.
and   because   particularly

_____

_____

5. That lime has vitamin C.
These lemons have vitamin C.
because   but   and

_____

_____

H Circle each bone that will move. Then draw an arrow that shows which way the bone will move.

I Write the conclusion of each deduction.

1. Feelings travel on sense nerves.
Pain is a feeling.

_____

_____

2. Commands go on motor nerves.
"Move arm" is a command.

_____

_____

3. Some diseases damage nerves.
Polio is a disease.

_____

_____

J Draw in the arrows. Shade in each tube that carries dark blood. Tell if each tube is a **vein** or an **artery**.

1. _____

2. _____

3. _____

4. _____

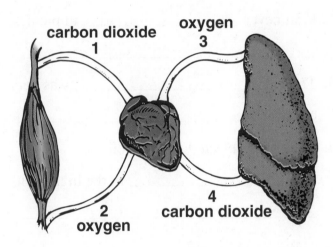

carbon dioxide
1

oxygen
3

2
oxygen

4
carbon dioxide

WORD LIST

Bronchial tubes (n) *means* the tubes inside the lungs.

Conclude (v) *means* end or figure out.

Conclusion (n) *means* the end or something that is concluded.

Examine (v) *means* look at.

Explain (v) *means* make something easier to understand.

Lung (n) *means* a large organ that brings air into contact with the blood.

Manufacture (v) *means* make in a factory.

Manufactured (a) *means* that something has been made in a factory.

Manufacturer (n) *means* something that manufactures.

Regulate (v) *means* control.

Reside (v) *means* live somewhere.

Respiratory system (n) *means* the body system that brings oxygen to the blood.

Select (v) *means* choose.

Trachea (n) *means* the tube that brings outside air to the lungs.

ERRORS | O | W | B | T

A Underline the contradiction.
Circle the statement it contradicts.
Tell **why** the underlined statement contradicts the circled statement.
Make the underlined statement true.

The Smiths had a wood stove in their kitchen. One night, their electricity went out. They all huddled together in the kitchen because the house was so cold. Mrs. Smith closed the doors and lit a fire in the stove. * Pretty soon, everybody was toasty warm. The kitchen air began to fill with carbon dioxide, so Mrs. Smith opened the doors. Then she turned on the lights.

_____

_____

B Write the instructions.

①
_____
liver   ③◯
②

1. _____

_____

2. _____

_____

_____

3. _____

_____

_____

C Write a word that comes from **participate** in each blank. Then write **verb, noun,** or **adjective** after each item.

1. He had a _____ role in the meeting. _____

2. Fran never _____ in picnics.

_____

3. Their _____ was very constructive. _____

4. The coach selected two players to _____ in the high jump.

_____

5. Those two girls are _____ in the parade. _____

D Tell which fact each statement relates to. Make each contradiction true.

| 1. The demand for pens was high. |
| 2. The supply of pens was low. |

a. Not very many people wanted pens.   _____

b. It was hard to find a pen.   _____

c. Stores had tons and tons of pens.   _____

E Fill in each blank.

1. _____

2. _____

3. _____

4. _____

5. _____

6. _____

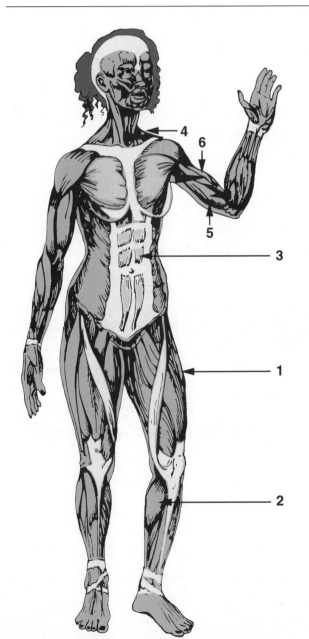

F Circle the word that combines the sentences correctly. Combine the sentences with that word.

1. The Bing Company manufactures baseballs.
   Smashers Unlimited manufactures baseballs.
   which   and   particularly

   _____

   _____

   _____

2. Mr. Brown is very critical.
   Mr. Brown is most critical when he is hungry.
   and   because   particularly

   _____

   _____

3. Diane is participating in the play.
   Vernon is participating in the play.
   particularly   but   and

   _____

   _____

4. Hector is wearing a hat.
   Hector doesn't like his haircut.
   but   which   because

   _____

   _____

   _____

5. The cheetah was faster than the jeep.
   The lion was faster than the jeep.
   which   and   particularly

   _____

   _____

G Read the story and answer the questions.
Circle the **W** if the question is answered by words in the story, and underline those words.
Circle the **D** if the question is answered by a deduction.

You know that when the demand is greater than the supply, prices go up. Mrs. Lopez runs the only chicken farm near Mudville. In March, her chickens produce just as many eggs as Mudville needs, which is 1000 dozen a month. Mrs. Lopez sells the eggs for $1 a dozen, so she makes $1000 that month. In April, a big group of people moves into Mudville, and Mudville's demand for eggs goes up to 1500 dozen a month. But Mrs. Lopez's chickens are still producing only 1000 dozen a month, and it becomes very hard for the people of Mudville to get all the eggs they need. People start to offer Mrs. Lopez more for her eggs, just so they can be sure of getting some. Mrs. Lopez, who likes the idea of making extra money, decides to raise the price by 25¢. Because the demand is so high, she has no trouble selling the eggs at the new price.

1. What's the rule about demand and supply?

_____

_____

_____

2. What was the price of eggs in February if the demand was the same as the supply?

_____ **W**   **D**

3. Was the demand greater than the supply because the supply went down or because the demand went up?

_____

_____ **W**   **D**

4. Why do people start offering Mrs. Lopez more for her eggs?

_____

_____ **W**   **D**

5. Why doesn't Mrs. Lopez have any trouble selling eggs at a new price?

_____

_____ **W**   **D**

6. Would prices have gone up if the chickens laid only 500 eggs in March?

_____ **W**   **D**

H Tell **two** ways that the things compared are **not** the same.
Tell **one** way that the things compared **are** the same.

Her criticism was like a razor.

1. _____

_____

2. _____

_____

3. _____

Read the story and answer the questions. Circle the **W** if the question is answered by words in the story, and underline those words.
Circle the **D** if the question is answered by a deduction.

Here's another rule about demand and supply: Manufacturers always try to make the demand greater than the supply. Mr. Franklin runs the only lightbulb factory in Mudville. In May, he produces just as many lightbulbs as Mudville needs, which is 1000 a month. Mr. Franklin makes 50¢ for each light bulb he sells that month. In June, Mr. Franklin decides that he wants to make more than 50¢ for each lightbulb he sells. He knows that if he can make the demand greater than the supply, the price of lightbulbs will go up. So he puts an ad in the paper that says, "If you have more lamps in your house, you will be able to see better. You won't stub your toes in dark corners, you will be able to read anywhere, and your house will be cheery." The ad works, and the demand for lightbulbs goes up. Because the demand is so high, Mr. Franklin raises the price of his lightbulbs, and he sells all 1000 of them.

1. What's another rule about demand and supply?

_____

_____

_____

2. How much money did Mr. Franklin make in May?

_____ W   D

3. What did the ad try to make people think?

_____

_____ W   D

4. Why is Mr. Franklin able to sell all 1000 of his light bulbs in June at the higher price?

_____

_____ W   D

5. Name another way that Mr. Franklin could have increased the demand.

_____

_____

6. What would happen to the demand if the ad did not work?

_____

_____ W   D

7. If Mr. Franklin makes 60¢ for each light bulb he sells in June, how much money will he make that month?

_____

B For each sentence, write **two** sentences that have the underlined common part.

1. Randy, who likes participatory sports, broke his leg playing basketball.

   a._____

   _____

   b._____

   _____

2. Ted has poor circulation because he smokes.

   a._____

   _____

   b._____

   _____

3. The woman felt bad, but she didn't go to the doctor.

   a._____

   _____

   b._____

   _____

4. Those new regulations are stupid and unfair.

   a._____

   _____

   b._____

   _____

C Rewrite the paragraph in four sentences on your own lined paper. If one of the sentences tells **why,** combine the sentences with **because.** If sentences seem contradictory, combine them with **but.**

Magellan tried to sail around the world. Magellan was born in 1480. He lived in Portugal. Portugal is next to Spain. Magellan tried to obtain ships in Portugal. Magellan did not have any luck. So Magellan went to see the Spanish king. The Spanish king gave him five ships.

D Tell **two** ways that the things compared are **not** the same.

Tell **one** way that the things compared **are** the same.

The house was a goldfish bowl.

1._____

_____

2._____

_____

3._____

_____

E Underline the contradiction. Circle the statement it contradicts. Tell **why** the underlined statement contradicts the circled statement. Make the underlined statement true.

Gina did many exercises every day. In her first exercise, she bent her arms to pick up big boxes. In her second exercise, she stood on her toes. In her third exercise, she turned her head. * She said, "These exercises are only good for my triceps, my gastrocnemius, and my trapezius. I need to start working on my abdominal muscles and my quadriceps." So she got an exercise book from the library.

_____

_____

F Label each nerve.
Write a message for each nerve.

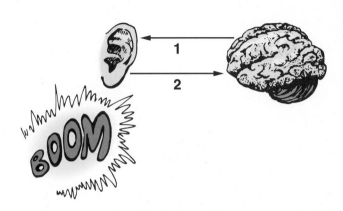

1. _____

2. _____

G Circle the subject and underline the predicate. Rewrite each sentence by moving part of the predicate.

1. You should wear big boots to go hiking.

_____

_____

2. They can play if they finish their homework.

_____

_____

3. Her dad drank milk before he went to work.

_____

_____

4. A plane was flying over the house.

_____

_____

H Fill in each blank.

1. _____

2. _____

3. _____

4. _____

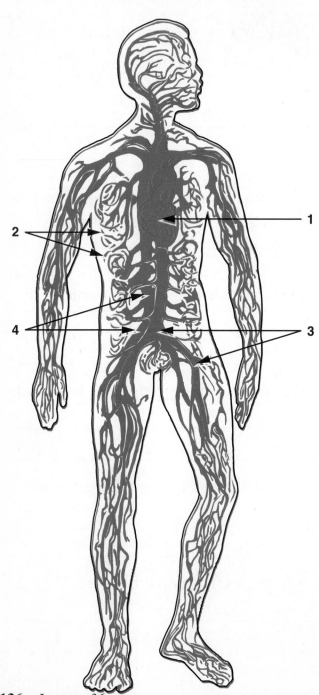

I Underline the nouns. Draw a line **over** the adjectives. Circle the verbs.

1. Participatory sports are played in every country.

2. Students are participating in that assembly.

3. A manufacturer in town was modifying some smokestacks.

4. The government regulates many manufacturers.

J Fill in the blank with the word that has the same meaning as the word or words under the blank.

1. Some _____ are more
      (things that are constructed)
than one hundred stories high.

2. Your body is always _____ new
                              (making)
blood cells.

3. Meat takes a long time to be

_____.
(changed into fuel for the body)

4. Earthquakes are hard to

_____.
(say that they will happen)

A Make up a simile for each item.

1. Her teeth were very white.

_____

_____

2. Her hair was very red.

_____

_____

B For each sentence, write **two** sentences that have the underlined common part.

1. Water is hard to find, particularly in deserts.

a. _____

_____

b. _____

_____

2. Tom and Roberto are skating on the pond.

a. _____

_____

b. _____

_____

3. You must follow this regulation, which states that you cannot smoke.

a. _____

_____

b. _____

_____

4. The man and the woman have been running for ten minutes.

a. _____

_____

b. _____

_____

C Circle the subject and underline the predicate. Rewrite each sentence by moving part of the predicate.

1. They planted a garden next to their residence.

_____

_____

2. Participation in sports is not important if you're sick.

_____

_____

3. He opened the tool chest by using a hammer.

_____

_____

4. She took out her wallet as she got on the bus.

_____

_____

D Read the story and answer the questions. Circle the **W** if the question is answered by words in the story, and underline those words. Circle the **D** if the question is answered by a deduction.

> **Your cerebellum had to learn how to work, but your medulla knew how to work when you were born. When you first started walking, your cerebrum had to think about every move you made with your walking muscles. As you became better at walking, your cerebellum took over more and more control of those walking muscles. Now you don't have to think about how to walk. The same thing happens every time you learn to do something new with your muscular system, such as playing basketball, dancing, or riding a bike. Your cerebrum controls things at first, but when you have learned how to move your muscles, your cerebellum takes over.**

1. What are the three parts of the brain?

_____

_____

2. What does your cerebellum have to learn?

_____ **W**   **D**

3. Which part controls the walking muscles at first?

_____ **W**   **D**

4. Which part controls the walking muscles later?

_____ **W**   **D**

5. Tell which part of the brain you use for the following things:

a. jumping _____

b. learning how to jump _____

c. thinking _____

d. doing sit-ups _____

e. heart beating _____

f. rolling over _____

E Fill in each blank.

1. _____

2. _____

3. _____

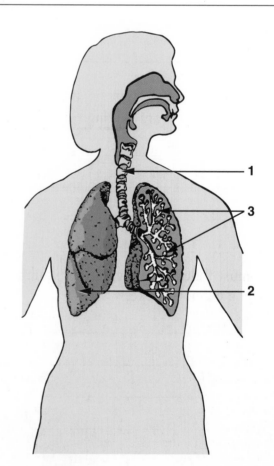

F Rewrite the paragraph in four sentences on your own lined paper. If one of the sentences tells **why,** combine the sentences with **because.** If sentences seem contradictory, combine them with **but.**

Magellan left Spain in 1519. Magellan crossed the Atlantic Ocean. In 1520, Magellan sailed into the Pacific Ocean through what is now the Strait of Magellan. The Strait of Magellan is a channel at the southern tip of South America. Magellan's crew began to get restless. Magellan's crew got the most restless when they were crossing the Pacific. Magellan's ships took several months to cross the Pacific Ocean. Magellan's ships were not very fast.

G Underline the contradiction. Circle the statement it contradicts. Tell **why** the underlined statement contradicts the circled statement. Make the underlined statement true.

Your leg has many veins. Some of these veins carry carbon dioxide away from your gastrocnemius. The farther they go up your leg, the bigger they get. * You can see some of these veins on some people if you look closely. These veins are easiest to see near the ankles. They look red, and some of them are very near the skin.

_____

_____

_____

H Fill in each blank with the word that has the same meaning as the word or words under the blank.

1. Many schools have fewer _____
   (rules)
   now than they had ten years ago.

2. Cars _____ fuel.
   (use up)

3. Some businesses _____ their
   (change)
   products every year.

4. Many companies _____
   (make in a factory)
   only one product.

I Underline the nouns. Draw a line **over** the adjectives. Circle the verbs.

1. Manufacturers are controlling the supply of car parts.

2. The teacher supplied his students with pencils for the test.

3. This product has a low demand.

4. The workers demanded some changes at the factory.

ERRORS | O | W | B | T

A Tell if each event changed the **demand** or the **supply.**

A farmer had 10,000 chickens.
A man obtained 500 chickens a week for his store.

1. A hailstorm killed a third of the chickens.

_____

2. Because of the hailstorm, the man from the store did not come to the farm.

_____

3. A man from another store came out and said that his store needed 100 chickens a week.

_____

4. The hens hatched 500 chickens the next week.

_____

B Make up a simile for each item.

1. The man was very tall.

_____

_____

2. Her skin was smooth.

_____

_____

C Underline the common part. For each sentence, write **two** sentences with that common part.

1. Blue River floods a lot, particularly in the spring.

a. _____

_____

b. _____

_____

2. One cup and six plates were on the table.

a. _____

_____

b. _____

_____

3. Ten dogs and six cats were running in the yard.

a. _____

_____

b. _____

_____

4. Lillian and James walk to work every day.

a. _____

_____

b. _____

_____

D Draw the arrow for each nerve.
Write a message for each nerve.

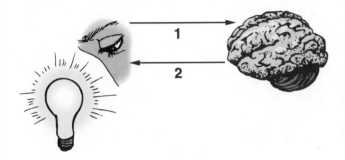

1. _____

2. _____

E Write the instructions.

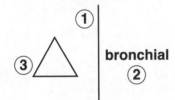

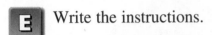

bronchial
②

1. _____

_____

2. _____

_____

_____

3. _____

_____

_____

F Use the facts to fill out the form.

**Facts: Your name is Mickey O'Hara.
You are applying for a loan to buy a
house. You work at the Johnson
Carpet Company. You make $2400 a
month. You are 28 years old and
married. You rent a house for $550 a
month. Your car payments are $220
a month. Mrs. O'Hara works in a
bakery and makes $1200 a month.
You drive a 1995 compact car.**

Instructions:

1. Type of loan needed: _____

2. Total monthly income in your household:

_____

3. Current employer: _____

_____

4. Age: _____

5. Model of car: _____

6. Year: _____

7. Total yearly payments on car: _____

8. Cross out the first sentence that gives
information you didn't use.

G Write **R** for each fact that is **relevant** to what happened. Write **I** for each fact that is **irrelevant** to what happened.

She will participate in the swim meet.

1. She wants to win a medal. _____

2. She swims in the lake. _____

3. She's been swimming every day. _____

4. She wears goggles when she swims. _____

H Fill in each blank.

1. _____

2. _____

3. _____

1 and 2. _____ nervous system

3. _____ nervous system

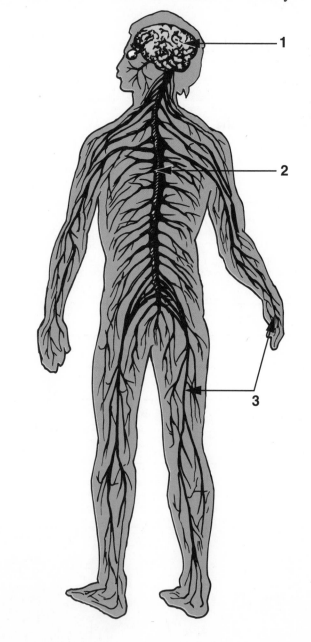

I Circle the word that combines the sentences correctly. Combine the sentences with that word.

1. A pickup truck was having a race.
A dirt bike was having a race.
particularly   which   and

_____

_____

2. Sense nerves send messages to the brain.
Sense nerves let you feel.
who   which   particularly

_____

_____

_____

3. That older woman has bad circulation.
Her youngest son has bad circulation.
who   which   and

_____

_____

_____

4. He respires loudly.
He respires most loudly when he has a cold.
because   particularly   which

_____

_____

_____

5. Tom predicts snow tonight.
His brothers predict snow tonight.
but   because   and

_____

_____

_____

J Underline the contradiction. Circle the statement it contradicts. Tell **why** the underlined statement contradicts the circled statement. Make the underlined statement true.

Sam resided in the suburbs and worked in the city. One day, he tripped over a wire at work. His lower leg was badly hurt. * Sam went to a doctor, who took X rays of Sam's leg. The doctor said that Sam had pulled his gastrocnemius, but that it wouldn't take long to heal. Sam went back to his home in the city and stayed in bed for a week.

_____

_____

A Underline the redundant sentences.

Some people read magazines. Some people don't. The store had many different kinds of magazines. John wanted to acquire a magazine, so he went to the store. The store had a wide selection of magazines. John looked for a magazine about cars. The store had ten different car magazines. John tried to decide which one to buy. The store had more than one car magazine. John didn't know which one he wanted.

B Write a word that comes from **circulate** or **respire** in each blank. Then write **verb, noun,** or **adjective** after each item.

1. The _____ system moves

   blood around the body. _____

2. The _____ system brings

   oxygen to the blood. _____

3. Your heart _____ blood.

   _____

4. He is _____ through his

   nose. _____

5. Her _____ is bad because

   her capillaries are clogged. _____

C Underline the common part. For each sentence, write **two** sentences with that common part.

1. People get many diseases, particularly in the winter.

   a. _____

   _____

   b. _____

   _____

2. The demand for gas, which is large, increases each year.

   a. _____

   _____

   b. _____

   _____

3. The doctor checked the man's respiration, which was loud.

   a. _____

   _____

   b. _____

   _____

4. Her mother and father are talking about money.

   a. _____

   _____

   b. _____

   _____

D Tell if each event changed the **demand** or the **supply**.

> **The factory manufactured 1000 cars a week.**
>
> **The factory sold 1000 cars a week.**

1. The power went out at the factory, and no cars were made for a week.

_____

2. For two weeks, people did not buy cars.

_____

3. The factory made 2000 cars in one week.

_____

4. People started buying the factory's cars again.

_____

E Make up a simile for each item.

1. His body was limp.

_____

_____

2. The dancer could spin very fast.

_____

_____

F Rewrite the story in four sentences on your own lined paper.

If one of the sentences tells **why**, combine the sentences with **because**.

If sentences seem contradictory, combine them with **but**.

> Finally, Magellan came to an island called Cebu. Cebu is in the southern Philippine Islands. Magellan thought that his trip was almost over. Magellan was still very far from home. Magellan was killed on Cebu. Magellan got into a fight. His crew fled Cebu. His crew kept on sailing.

G Write the instructions.

① ◯ □ ③

circulation
②

1. _____

_____

2. _____

_____

3. _____

_____

H Circle the subject and underline the predicate. Rewrite each sentence by moving part of the predicate.

1. She respired deeply because she felt dizzy.

_____

_____

2. Everyone was cold last winter.

_____

_____

3. Many people walk quickly in New York.

_____

_____

4. The Golden Gate Bridge must be painted every year.

_____

_____

I Make each statement mean the same thing as the statement in the box.

> **Jenny, who participated in many sports, was very strong.**

1. Jenny, who took part in many sports, wasn't very strong.
2. Jenny, who had lots of strength, took part in many sports.
3. Jenny participated in many sports and was very strong.
4. Jenny was very strong, and she didn't take part in many sports.

J Use the facts to fill out the form.

> **Facts: You are applying for a job in a department store. You want to sell dresses, but you will also work as a cashier. You have worked as a cashier for three years at Snappy Burger, and you are bored with the job. You have never had a serious illness. You live at 22 Madrona Court in Los Angeles, California. Your social security number is 123-12-0888. Your name is Susan Thompson.**

Instructions:
   a. On line 8, write your social security number.
   b. On line 4, state how many years you have held your present job.
   c. Write your first name on line 3.
   d. On line 2, tell what state you live in.
   e. List any serious illnesses you have had on line 7.
   f. Print your street address on line 6.
   g. Tell what job you want most on line 5.
   h. Print the name of your current employer on line 1.

1. _____

2. _____

3. _____

4. _____

5. _____

6. _____

7. _____

8. _____

K Draw in the arrows. Shade in each tube that carries dark blood. Tell what gas each tube carries.

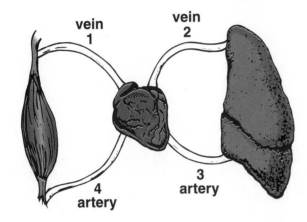

1. _____

2. _____

3. _____

4. _____

WORD LIST

Construct (v) *means* **build.**

Consumable (a) *means* that something can be consumed.

Consumer (n) *means* something that consumes.

Demand (n) *means* how well something sells.

Manufacture (v) *means* make in a factory.

Modified (a) *means* that something is changed.

Obtain (v) *means* get.

Participate (v) *means* take part in something.

Participation (n) *means* the act of participating.

Participatory (a) *means* that something involves participation.

Predicate (n) *means* the part of a sentence that tells more.

Predict (v) *means* say that something will happen.

Subject (n) *means* the part of a sentence that names.

Supply (n) *means* how much there is of something.

ERRORS	O	W	B	T

A Underline the common part. For each sentence, write **two** sentences with that common part.

1. The movie was predictable, but it was funny.

   a. _____

   _____

   b. _____

   _____

2. The teacher and his students have gone home.

   a. _____

   _____

   b. _____

   _____

3. She participated in the play and produced a film.

   a. _____

   _____

   b. _____

   _____

4. Fred respires loudly because he has a cold.

   a. _____

   _____

   b. _____

   _____

B Answer the questions.

1. What's the rule about when the demand is greater than the supply?

   _____

   _____

   _____

   In the winter, the demand for grapes is greater than the supply of grapes.

2. What will happen to the price of grapes?

   _____

3. How do you know?

   _____

   _____

   Last summer, the price of bikes went up.

4. Which was greater, the demand or the supply?

   _____

5. How do you know?

   _____

   _____

   This year, the demand for gas is greater than the supply of gas.

6. What will happen to the price of gas?

   _____

7. How do you know?

_____

_____

 Underline the redundant sentences.

A bell rang. Sam put on his fire fighter's hat and his fire fighter's coat. He jumped on the fire truck as it roared out of the station. Sam was a fire fighter. The truck sped down Oak Street and screeched around the corner of Oak and First. The truck was going sixty miles an hour. The truck was going fast. At First and Elm, the truck screamed to a stop, and Sam jumped off to look for a fire hydrant. The fire was at First and Elm.

D Read the story and answer the questions. Circle the **W** if the question is answered by words in the story, and underline those words. Circle the **D** if the question is answered by a deduction.

When you stub your toe, the message "Toe hurts" goes from your toe to your brain. Your nerves don't really carry the words "Toe hurts." What they do carry is a little bit of electricity. The electricity comes in very short bursts called impulses. If the toe doesn't hurt too much, the message may have thirty impulses per second. If the toe hurts a lot, the message may have more than 100 impulses per second. The greater the pain, the more impulses per second.

1. Which system carries the message "Toe hurts" to your brain?

_____ **W** **D**

2. How is a nerve like a lamp cord?

_____

_____ **W** **D**

3. What are impulses?

_____

_____

4. If a message has 10 impulses per second, how many impulses will it have in five seconds?

_____

5. Message A has 50 impulses per second. Message B has 120 impulses per second. Which message carries more pain?

_____ **W** **D**

6. Which gives more impulses per second, banging your knee against a door or touching your knee with a glove?

_____

_____

7. Which gives more impulses per second, touching your finger with a feather or cutting your finger with a knife?

_____

_____

E Rewrite the story in four sentences on your own lined paper. If one of the sentences tells **why,** combine the sentences with **because.** If sentences seem contradictory, combine them with **but.**

In 1522, Magellan's crew arrived in Spain. Spain looked good to them. Five ships had started the trip. Only one ship finished the trip. The crew had acquired many things. The crew acquired mostly spices. People paid a lot of money for the spices. The spices were very rare.

F Write the instructions.

③
regulation
①
digestion
②

1. _____

   _____

2. _____

   _____

3. _____

   _____

G Make up a simile for each item.

1. She can sing very well.

   _____

   _____

2. His voice is very loud.

   _____

   _____

H Write a word that comes from **circulate** or **respire** in each blank. Then write **verb, noun,** or **adjective** after each item.

1. You have to _____ to get air into your lungs. _____

2. _____ is the act of breathing.

   _____

3. Publishers _____ many books. _____

4. Your lungs are in your _____ system. _____

5. Some people enjoy _____ at parties. _____

1 Underline the contradiction. Circle the statement it contradicts. Tell **why** the underlined statement contradicts the circled statement. Make the underlined statement true.

Joan was a very productive painter. She had more than a hundred pictures ready for an art show, and she was very excited. One day when she was working, a pot of paint fell on her hand and hurt the motor nerves in her fingers. * Joan went to see a doctor. He knew that she was an artist who painted lots of things. He told her that she would still be able to move her fingers, but that she wouldn't feel anything with them for a while. Joan felt lucky.

_____

_____

ERRORS | O | W | B | T

A Answer the questions.

1. What's the rule about when the demand is greater than the supply?

_____

_____

_____

In the fall, the demand for warm coats is greater than the supply of warm coats.

2. What will happen to the price of warm coats?

_____

3. How do you know?

_____

_____

Last year, the price of gasoline went up.

4. Which was greater, the supply or the demand?

_____

5. How do you know?

_____

_____

Fifty people want to buy swimsuits.

The seller has thirty swimsuits.

6. Which is greater, the supply or the demand?

_____

7. What will happen to the price of swimsuits?

_____

8. How do you know?

_____

_____

B Underline the redundant sentences.

Jane was on a low-calorie diet. She ate only peaches. Jane wanted to lose weight. Jane became very weak and sick because she wasn't getting all the vitamins and minerals she needed. The doctor gave Jane some vitamin pills. Jane took the pills. The pills were full of vitamins. She felt better and lost ten pounds. After she started taking the pills, Jane lost weight.

C Combine the sentences with **although**.

1. John went to school.
   John wanted to stay at home.

   _____

   _____

   _____

2. Sam constructs many things.
   Sam doesn't have any tools.

   _____

   _____

   _____

3. Jane was hungry.
   Jane didn't want to eat.

   _____

   _____

D Read the story and answer the questions.
   Circle the W if the question is answered
   by words in the story, and underline
   those words. Circle the D if the question
   is answered by a deduction.

Here's another rule about demand and supply: When the demand is less than the supply, prices go down. Mrs. Thomas runs the only dairy farm near Newton. In July, her cows produce just as much milk as Newton needs, which is 1000 gallons a month. In August, a big group of people moves out of Newton, and Newton's demand for milk drops to 600 gallons a month. But Mrs. Thomas's cows are still producing 1000 gallons a month. She sells 600 gallons at the old price, and then she is stuck with 400 gallons that will soon go bad. Mrs. Thomas thinks that she can get people to buy the 400 gallons if she lowers the price. Her idea works, and she sells all 400 gallons at the lower price.

1. What's another rule about demand and supply?

   _____

   _____

   _____

2. What would have happened to the price of milk if a big group of people had moved into Newton in July?

   _____

   _____ W   D

3. Was the demand smaller than the supply in August because the demand went down or because the supply went up?

_____

_____

4. What does Mrs. Thomas do to get people to buy the 400 gallons she had left over?

_____ **W**   **D**

5. What does Mrs. Thomas have to do to the demand to sell 1000 gallons at the old price in September?

_____ **W**   **D**

6. Name one way she could do that.

_____

_____

7. Did Mrs. Thomas lose money in August?

_____ **W**   **D**

E Underline the common part. For each sentence, write two sentences with that common part.

1. America and Japan manufacture cars.

a. _____

_____

b. _____

_____

2. A goat and its kids are consuming those bushes.

a. _____

_____

b. _____

_____

3. Turkeys are stupid, particularly when they're young.

a. _____

_____

b. _____

_____

4. Six women and a boy were constructing a swimming pool.

a. _____

_____

b. _____

_____

F Write a word that comes from **manufacture** or **participate** in each blank. Then write **verb, noun,** or **adjective** after each item.

1. A car _____ has to follow regulations. _____

2. Some companies don't _____ many products. _____

3. You don't have to _____ in this game. _____

4. Many _____ products are advertised. _____

5. Some classes are not very _____.

_____

G Underline the contradiction. Circle the statement it contradicts. Tell **why** the underlined statement contradicts the circled statement. Make the underlined statement true.

When Mel finished high school, he left Columbus for a year. While he was away, construction workers modified every building on Main Street. Many people moved into town, and the mayor had to make new regulations. Most people predicted that Columbus would keep growing. * When Mel came back, he hardly recognized the place. All kinds of new people were walking in the streets. His friends were saying that Columbus would get bigger. There were many new rules to follow. At least the barber shop on Main Street was the same.

_____

_____

H Tell which fact each statement relates to. Make each contradiction true.

1. **The demand for bottles was low.**
2. **The supply of bottles was high.**

a. Many people wanted bottles. _____

b. Stores had very few bottles. _____

c. It was easy to find bottles. _____

I Write the conclusion of each deduction.

1. Commands come from the brain. "Bend knee" is a command.

_____

_____

2. Some diseases damage your heart. Measles is a disease.

_____

_____

3. Feelings go to the brain. Cold is a feeling.

_____

_____

J Follow the directions.

1. Draw a big circle.
2. Draw a horizontal line from the left side of the circle to the right side of the circle.
3. Draw a vertical line from the top of the circle to the bottom of the circle.
4. In the top right part of the circle, write the word that means **use up** or **eat.**

K Tell **two** ways that the things compared are **not** the same. Tell **one** way that the things compared **are** the same.

The field was a pancake.

1. _____

   _____

2. _____

   _____

3. _____

   _____

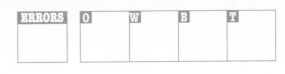
A Cross out the wrong word and write the correct word above it.　　**(4)**

Last year, Mike have three rabbits. He kept them in a cage. One night, the rabbits got out of the cage. It hopped under the house and wouldn't come out. Mike had to crawl under the house to grab her rabbits. He pulled them out by the ears and put it back in the cage.

 B Combine the sentences with **although**.

1. That car is new.
That car is not running.

_____

_____

2. She consumed lots of food.
She did not get fat.

_____

_____

_____

3. Tod likes to go fast.
Tod hates jets.

_____

_____

C Answer the questions.

1. What's the rule about when the demand is greater than the supply?

_____

_____

_____

Chong's Meat Market raised the price of turkey yesterday.

2. Which was greater, the supply or the demand?

_____

3. How do you know?

_____

_____

Twenty people want turkeys. Chong's Meat Market has ten turkeys.

4. Which is greater, the supply or the demand?

_____

5. What will happen to the price of turkey?

_____

Last week, turkeys cost 40¢ a pound.
This week, turkeys cost 50¢ a pound.

6. What happened to the price of turkeys?

_____

7. Which was greater, the supply or the demand?

_____

8. How do you know?

_____

D Write the middle part of each deduction.

1. The company manufactured products.

_____

So, maybe the company manufactured tires.

2. Feelings go to the brain.

_____

So, heat goes to the brain.

3. Muscles do not push.

_____

So, the trapezius does not push.

E Write a word that comes from **predict** or **digest** in each blank. Then write **verb, noun,** or **adjective** after each item.

1. He _____ that we would

have a cold winter. _____

2. The way she acts is always _____.

_____

3. Some people get tired when they _____

lots of food. _____

4. Being well helps your _____.

_____

5. _____ sometimes come true.

_____

F Underline the redundant sentences.

Donna was a paper clip manufacturer. She made paper clips in a factory. Every day Donna got up at 6 A.M. and went to her factory. She made sure that the factory workers were doing their jobs. She got up very early in the morning. Donna liked her factory. It was clean and modern. Her workers were happy because she paid them a lot of money. Every afternoon at 3 P.M., the workers had a paper clip fight. Then they went back to work. The factory workers were happy because they got good pay checks. Donna was happy because her workers were happy.

G Follow the directions.

1. Write a big **T.**
2. On the right side of the **T,** write the word that means **make something in a factory.**
3. On the left side of the **T,** write what part of speech that word is.
4. Draw a horizontal line under the **T.**

H Underline the common part. For each sentence, write two sentences with that common part.

1. Redwoods get very big, particularly in California.

   a. _____

   _____

   b. _____

   _____

2. Mike and Kim have many secrets.

   a. _____

   _____

   b. _____

   _____

3. That company, which manufactures paper, hires a lot of people.

   a. _____

   _____

   b. _____

   _____

4. Gloria modified her stereo, which had large speakers.

   a. _____

   _____

   b. _____

   _____

I Write what each analogy tells.

What each word means
What part of speech each word is
What adjective comes from each word
What noun comes from each word

1. **Manufacture** is to **make in a factory** as **participate** is to **take part in something.**

   _____

   _____

2. **Manufacture** is to **manufacturer** as **participate** is to **participation.**

   _____

   _____

3. **Manufacture** is to **manufactured** as **participate** is to **participatory.**

   _____

   _____

LESSON 42

J Read the story and answer the questions. Circle the **W** if the question is answered by words in the story, and underline those words. Circle the **D** if the question is answered by a deduction.

> You know that when the demand is less than the supply, prices go down. Mr. Hightower runs the only chicken farm near Newton. In September, his chickens produce just as many eggs as Newton needs, which is 1000 dozen a month. Mr. Hightower sells the eggs for $2 a dozen, so he makes $2000 that month. The people of Newton think that $2 a dozen is too much to pay for eggs. In October, they all get together and decide not to buy eggs from Mr. Hightower. This is called a boycott. Mr. Hightower, whose chickens are still producing eggs, is stuck with 1000 dozen eggs that will soon go bad. The only way he can make any money in October is to lower the price of eggs and hope that people will like the new price. So he lowers the price to $1 a dozen. The people of Newton like this new price, and they buy all the eggs.

1. What's the rule?

   _____

   _____

   _____

2. Why do people decide not to buy eggs in October?

   _____

   _____

   _____

3. Why is Mr. Hightower stuck with 1000 dozen eggs?

   _____

   _____

   _____ **W**   **D**

4. Was the demand smaller than the supply because the demand went down or because the supply went up?

   _____

   _____ **W**   **D**

5. Why did Mr. Hightower lower the price?

   _____

   _____

6. How much did Mr. Hightower make in October?

   _____

7. What does a boycott do to the demand?

   _____ **W**   **D**

A Write the instructions.

③ productive ② production

①

1. _____

_____

2. _____

_____

3. _____

_____

B Combine the sentences with **although**.

1. Brian ate a lot of food.
   Brian was not hungry.

   _____

   _____

2. Kathy went on a diet.
   Kathy did not get any thinner.

   _____

   _____

   _____

3. Bianca was tired.
   Bianca didn't sleep.

   _____

   _____

C Answer the questions.

1. What's the rule about when the demand is greater than the supply?

   _____

   _____

   _____

2. What's the rule about what manufacturers try to do?

   _____

   _____

   _____

3. Why do manufacturers try to do that?

   _____

   _____

> **A car manufacturer makes 1000 cars a week and sells 1000 cars a week.**

4. Is the demand greater than the supply?

   _____

5. So what will the manufacturer try to do?

   _____

   _____

> **Name two ways that the manufacturer can do that.**

6. _____

7. _____

D For each sentence followed by a blank, write in the number of the rule that relates to that sentence.

> 1. **Hot air holds more water than cold air.**
> 2. **When hot air rises, it cools off.**

Very warm air blows across the ocean toward the West Coast of the United States. When it reaches the coast, the air is carrying a great deal of water. _____ It is then forced up because of the mountains along the coast. By the time it reaches the mountaintops, the air is quite cool. _____ The air can no longer hold all its water. _____ As a result, there is a lot of rain on the west side of the mountains. When the air goes down the east side of the mountains, it gets warmer. _____

E Cross out the wrong word and write the correct word above it.   **(4)**

That company manufacture animal crackers every day. The people who work there make cookie batter in big vats. Then they pour the batter into little molds of lions, tigers, and bears. After the batter is cooked, the animal crackers is rolled down a big belt. Workers stands at the belt. They throw away all the animal crackers that doesn't look like animals.

F Fill in each blank with the word that has the same meaning as the word or words under the blank.

1. They _____ a car
   (chose)
   with a large trunk.

2. Some people tried to figure out the

   _____ of that book.
   (end)

3. The worker _____ the company's
   (found fault with)
   plan.

4. Teachers should be able to

   _____.
   (make things easier to understand)

G Label each nerve as a **sense** nerve or a **motor** nerve. Draw an arrow to show which way the message moves.

1. "Hand itches."   2. "Rub towel on leg."

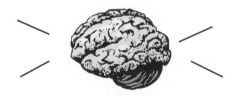

3. "Shoes are tight."   4. "Lips are chapped."

H Rewrite the paragraph in four sentences on your own lined paper. If one of the sentences tells **why,** combine the sentences with **because.** If sentences seem contradictory, combine them with **but.**

Diamonds and coal are made of the same mineral. The same mineral is carbon. Diamonds are used for jewelry. Diamonds are used in industry. Diamonds can cut any other material in the world. Diamonds are very hard. Some colored diamonds are quite rare. Red diamonds are the rarest.

I Underline the redundant sentences.

Only one of Jack's many friends had red hair. Most of Jack's friends did not have red hair. Jack's best friend, Bert, who had red hair, came over to Jack's home. Jack was downtown, looking for Bert. But Bert was at Jack's residence. Jack decided to go back to his home, and Bert decided to go downtown. They were changing places. Finally, Jack ran into Hector. Hector was not Jack's best friend. Hector did not have red hair.

J Fill in each blank.

1. _____

2. _____

3. _____

4. _____

5. _____

6. _____

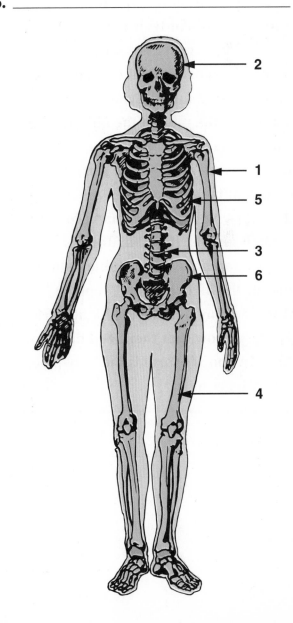

Read the story and answer the questions. Circle the **W** if the question is answered by words in the story, and underline those words. Circle the **D** if the question is answered by a deduction.

Here's a rule about demand and supply: When the demand is greater than the supply, prices go up. Mr. Jones runs the only dairy farm near Mudville. In January, his cows produce just as much milk as Mudville needs. Mr. Jones makes $1000 from milk sales that month. In February, his cows produce a lot less milk than Mudville needs. If Mr. Jones sells the milk at the old price, he won't make $1000 because he doesn't have as much milk to sell. But Mr. Jones wants to make $1000, so he raises his prices. Mudville's demand for milk is much greater than Mr. Jones's supply, and he has no trouble selling his milk at the higher price. People in Mudville may not like the higher price, but they know that they need milk, and that Mr. Jones's farm is the only place they can get milk.

1. What's the rule about demand and supply?

_____

_____

_____

2. Was the demand greater than the supply in January?

_____ **W**   **D**

3. Which was greater in February, the demand or the supply?

_____ **W**   **D**

4. If Mr. Jones sells his milk at the old price, why won't he make $1000?

_____

_____ **W**   **D**

5. Why did he raise his prices?

_____

_____

6. Why doesn't he have any trouble selling the milk at the higher price?

_____

_____

_____ **W**   **D**

7. Give two reasons why the people of Mudville pay the higher price, even though they don't like it.

a. _____

_____

b. _____

_____

_____

8. Did the demand get greater than the supply because the supply went down or because the demand went up?

_____

_____

ERRORS O W B T

A For each sentence followed by a blank, write in the number of the rule that relates to that sentence.

> 1. **When the demand is greater than the supply, prices go up.**
> 2. **Manufacturers try to make the demand greater than the supply.**

Not long ago, people did not want to buy bikes. They liked their cars, and they did not see any reason to own a bike. But when gas got expensive, the bike makers said, "A bike never needs gas." _____ Many people liked the idea of not paying for gas, and the demand for bikes skyrocketed. Prices soared. _____ Bike manufacturers had to work overtime just to meet the demand. When gas became cheap again, bike makers said, "If you buy a bike now, you will get a free lock." _____ The bike makers hoped that the lock gimmick would work. If enough people wanted a lock, the manufacturers could raise the price. _____

B Underline the redundant sentences.

Most people like to play sports. Some people don't. People who lived thousands of years ago had footraces. They had games to see who could throw a spear the farthest. They had games to see who could run the fastest. Today, we play basketball, football, and many other games. People played sports thousands of years ago. People will still be playing and watching sports thousands of years from now. There will be sports fans in the future.

C Write the instructions.

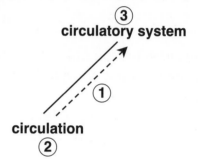

1. _____

_____

2. _____

_____

3. _____

_____

_____

D Answer the questions.

1. What's the rule about when the demand is greater than the supply?

_____

_____

_____

2. What's the rule about what manufacturers try to do?

_____

_____

_____

3. Why do manufacturers try to do that?

_____

A purse manufacturer makes 5000 purses a month and sells 4000 purses a month.

4. Is the demand greater than the supply?

_____

5. So what will the manufacturer try to do?

_____

_____

Name two ways that the manufacturer can do that.

6. _____

7. _____

E Combine the sentences with **although.**

1. He didn't have all the facts.
His conclusion was correct.

_____

_____

2. That regulation is not fair.
That regulation has to be followed.

_____

_____

_____

3. Clarence modified his engine.
His engine still doesn't run well.

_____

_____

_____

F Make up a simile for each item.

1. His feet are big.

_____

_____

2. Her hair was red.

_____

_____

G Cross out the wrong word and write the correct word above it.   **(4)**

One day, Tom were in a race and hurt his gastrocnemius. It hurt so badly that Tom can't walk. They had to stay in a hospital for two days. Then Tom got a cast on their leg. He couldn't run in any races for two months.

H Rewrite the paragraph in four sentences on your own lined paper. If one of the sentences tells **why,** combine the sentences with **because.** If sentences seem contradictory, combine them with **but.**

The Amazon River is the second longest river in the world. The Amazon River runs through South America. It is almost 4000 miles long. It is up to 300 feet deep. Many places along the river have bad floods. Many places along the river have the worst floods between January and June. You must be very careful when you fish in the Amazon River. The Amazon River has many alligators and dangerous fish.

I Underline the nouns. Draw a line over the adjectives. Circle the verbs.

1. The local paper has a large circulation.

2. Ten running women were respiring at a rapid rate.

3. Her heart is being examined.

4. Every written sentence must have an end mark.

J Use the facts to fill out the form.

Facts: Your name is Brian Ozaki. You have just graduated from State University in Rushville, with a B.A. degree in journalism. You are applying for a job with a newspaper. You were editor of your high school and college newspapers. You are twenty-two years old. You are single and unemployed. Your address is 22 W. Main, Farmington, NM. You want to write for the sports page.

Instructions:

1. Name, last name first (please print):

_____

2. Colleges or universities attended:

_____

3. Degrees, if any:

_____

4. Journalism experience, if any:

_____

_____

5. Current employer:

_____

6. Are you married? _____

7. Address: _____

_____

8. What section do you prefer to write for?

_____

WORD LIST

Carbon dioxide (n) *means* a gas that burning things produce.

Circulate (v) *means* move around.

Circulation (n) *means* the act of circulating.

Circulatory (a) *means* that something involves circulation.

Criticize (v) *means* find fault with.

Digestive (a) *means* that something involves digestion.

Explanation (n) *means* something that explains.

Oxygen (n) *means* a gas that burning things need.

Participate (v) *means* take part in something.

Produce (v) *means* make.

Redundant (a) *means* that something repeats what has already been said.

Respiration (n) *means* the act of respiring.

Respiratory (a) *means* that something involves respiration.

Respire (v) *means* breathe.

ERRORS | O | W | B | T

A Underline the redundant sentences.

Carla was writing a story. Her first sentence said, "The woman ran like the wind." Carla showed that the woman ran fast. Then she wrote five more sentences about the woman. Her story was six sentences long. Carla liked her story, so she let Dan read it. Dan read Carla's story. He said, "This is good, Carla. You should let other people read it." Carla liked her story, too. She told Dan that she would work on the story some more.

B For each sentence followed by a blank, write in the number of the rule that relates to that sentence.

1. **Unlike magnetic poles attract one another.**
2. **Like magnetic poles repel one another.**

All magnets have two poles, one on each end of the magnet. The two poles of the magnet are called the north pole and the south pole. If the magnet is shaped like a bar, one end of the bar is the north pole, and the other end is the south pole. If you hold the north pole of one magnet near the north pole of another magnet, the magnets will push against each other and try to move away from each other. _____ And if

you hold the south pole of one magnet against the south pole of another magnet, the magnets will try to move away from each other. _____ But if you hold the south pole of one magnet near the north pole of another magnet, the magnets will pull toward each other. _____ The magnets will stick together, and you will have to pull hard to separate them. _____

C

fist	**rock**

1. Tell how the objects could be the same.

_____

_____

2. Write a simile about the objects.

_____

_____

D Answer the questions.

1. What's the rule about when the demand is less than the supply?

_____

_____

2. What's the rule about what manufacturers try to do?

_____

_____

3. What's the rule about when the demand is greater than the supply?

_____

_____

_____

In the summer, the demand for grapes is less than the supply of grapes.

4. What will happen to the price of grapes?

_____

5. How do you know?

_____

_____

Last winter, the price of bikes went down.

6. Which was greater, the demand or the supply?

_____

7. How do you know?

_____

_____

8. What will the bike manufacturer try to do?

_____

_____

Name two ways that the manufacturer can do that.

9. _____

10. _____

E Circle the subject and underline the predicate. Rewrite each sentence by moving the predicate.

1. Many birds fly south every year.

_____

_____

2. Winters are drier in the Southwest.

_____

_____

3. She explained her criticism when Terry got mad.

_____

_____

4. He ate lots of carrots because he had night blindness.

_____

_____

F Underline the common part. For each sentence, write two sentences with that common part.

1. Although that manufacturer resides in a big house, she drives an old car.

   a. _____

   _____

   b. _____

   _____

2. Cops and dogs protected the residence from robbers.

   a. _____

   _____

   b. _____

   _____

3. A cop and his dog are protecting the home.

   a. _____

   _____

   b. _____

   _____

4. Jane consumed a lot of water because she was thirsty.

   a. _____

   _____

   b. _____

   _____

G Circle the word that combines the sentences correctly. Combine the sentences with that word.

1. Margie obtained a watch.

   Margie can't tell time.

   particularly   although   which

   _____

   _____

2. Blood circulates in your arteries.

   Nutrients circulate in your arteries.

   who   and   but

   _____

   _____

3. Jupiter has many moons.

   Saturn has many moons.

   although   because   and

   _____

   _____

4. Supply is related to prices.

   Demand is related to prices.

   although   and   which

   _____

   _____

5. Mrs. Ortega was digging for gold.

Her crew was digging for gold.

and   who   particularly

_____

_____

H   Use the facts to fill out the form.

> **Facts: Your name is Edna Vacek. You are applying for unemployment benefits. You were laid off last week by the Bunyan Lumber Company, where you worked the saw. You started working there five years ago, right after you finished high school. Your social security number is 999-42-6857. You want to get another job with a lumber company, and you will not take less than $300 a week. You are twenty-three years old.**

1. Name and age: _____

2. Social security number: _____

3. Circle highest school grade completed:

1   2   3   4   5   6   7   8   9   10   11   12

4. What kind of work are you looking for?

_____

5. What is the minimum starting wage you will accept on your next job?

_____

6. Who was your last employer?

_____

7. How long did you work there?

_____

8. How long have you been out of work?

_____

I   Cross out the wrong word and write the correct word above it.   **(5)**

> Last Monday, three men was running a race. They all had sneakers on. The man in the lead were wearing red shorts. Her hair was red also. He said to himself, "If I wins this race, I will get lots of money." So she ran faster. He won the race, but not by much.

ERRORS | O | W | B | T

A Answer the questions.

1. What's the rule about when the demand is greater than the supply?

_____

_____

_____

2. What's the rule about when the demand is less than the supply?

_____

_____

3. What's the rule about what manufacturers try to do?

_____

_____

_____

In the winter, the demand for mittens is greater than the supply of mittens.

4. What will happen to the price of mittens?

_____

5. How do you know?

_____

_____

This spring, mittens cost $1 a pair.
Last winter, mittens cost $2 a pair.

6. What happened to the price of mittens?

_____

7. Which was greater in the spring, the demand or the supply?

_____

8. How do you know?

_____

_____

9. What will mitten manufacturers try to do?

_____

_____

Name two ways that the manufacturers can do that.

10. _____

11. _____

B

neck   tree trunk

1. Tell how the objects could be the same.

_____

_____

2. Write a simile about the objects.

_____

_____

C For each sentence followed by a blank, write in the number of the rule that relates to that sentence.

1. **Vibrating objects produce sound.**
2. **Metals conduct sound better than air.**

Even when a train doesn't blow its whistle, it makes a lot of noise. It makes noise because all its parts are moving back and forth. _____ If you put a microphone next to the tracks, it can hear a train that is a mile away. If you put the microphone on the tracks, it can hear a train that is many miles away. _____ Sometimes the track, which is shaking, makes a little hum of its own. _____ In the old days, train robbers needed to know when a train was coming. Instead of listening for the sound in the air, they put their ears on the track. _____ They were always ready for the train when it came.

D Cross out the wrong word and write the correct word above it. **(5)**

Only a few years ago, people don't think it was important for girls to play sports. Schools had sports programs for boys, but not for girls. Today, people know that it are important for girls to play sports, too. Girls has basketball teams and baseball teams. Them run track and play volleyball. Playing sports is as good for girls as it are for boys.

E Underline the contradiction. Circle the statement it contradicts. Tell **why** the underlined statement contradicts the circled statement. Make the underlined statement true.

Corn farmers have to protect their crops from many different bugs. Many times in the past, bugs have wiped out corn crops. Last year, bugs ate a lot of corn, and there was not enough corn for everybody who wanted it. The farmers tried everything to get rid of the bugs. * They sprayed powder from planes. They tried to find animals that would eat the bugs. Corn prices began to go down. One company started manufacturing seeds that were bugproof. All in all, it was a very bad year for farmers.

_____

_____

_____

F Underline the redundant sentences.

Last summer, everybody in Coal City wanted a pair of sandals. Mr. Poole ran the only shoe store in town. There was a big demand for sandals. Mr. Poole got lots of sandals from a manufacturer. No other place in town sold sandals. Mr. Poole made $1 on each pair of sandals that he sold. One day, Mr. Poole sold 90 pairs of sandals. He made $90 from sandal sales that day. Every person in town wanted sandals.

G Read the story and answer the questions. Circle the W if the question is answered by words in the story, and underline those words. Circle the D if the question is answered by a deduction.

You know that when the demand is greater than the supply, prices go up. Mrs. Lopez runs the only chicken farm near Mudville. In March, her chickens produce just as many eggs as Mudville needs, which is 1000 dozen a month. Mrs. Lopez sells the eggs for $1 a dozen, so she makes $1000 that month. In April, a big group of people moves into Mudville, and Mudville's demand for eggs goes up to 1500 dozen a month. But Mrs. Lopez's chickens are still producing only 1000 dozen a month, and it becomes very hard for the people of Mudville to get all the eggs they need. People start to offer Mrs. Lopez more for her eggs, just so they can be sure of getting some. Mrs. Lopez, who likes the idea of making extra money, decides to raise the price by 25¢. Because the demand is so high, she has no trouble selling the eggs at the new price.

1. What's the rule about demand and supply?

_____

_____

_____

2. What was the price of eggs in February if the demand was the same as the supply?

_____ W   D

3. Was the demand greater than the supply because the supply went down or because the demand went up?

_____

_____ W   D

4. Why do people start offering Mrs. Lopez more for her eggs?

_____

_____ W   D

5. Why doesn't Mrs. Lopez have any trouble selling eggs at a new price?

_____

_____ W   D

6. Would prices have gone up if the chickens only laid 500 dozen eggs in March?

_____ W   D

H Underline the common part. For each sentence, write two sentences with that common part.

1. Although Don hurt his gastrocnemius, he can still run.

   a. _____

   _____

   b. _____

   _____

2. Frank and Martha participate on the volleyball team.

   a. _____

   _____

   b. _____

   _____

3. Her circulation, which is slow, is being checked by a doctor.

   a. _____

   _____

   b. _____

   _____

4. Roller coasters are fun, particularly when they are high.

   a. _____

   _____

   b. _____

   _____

I Tell what gas each tube carries. Shade in each tube that carries dark blood. Tell if each tube is a vein or an artery.

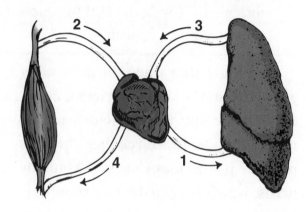

1. _____

2. _____

3. _____

4. _____

J Circle the word that combines the sentences correctly. Combine the sentences with that word.

1. Tom has been playing tennis.

   Bob has been playing tennis.

   which   and   but

   _____

   _____

2. Mary cut herself.

   Mary did not bleed.

   who   because   although

   _____

   _____

   _____

3. A captain is modifying that boat.

   His first mate is modifying that boat.

   although   but   and

   _____

   _____

   _____

4. The beginning of the film was predictable.

   The end of the film was predictable.

   who   particularly   and

   _____

   _____

   _____

5. Frank is selective.

   Frank is the most selective when he goes to restaurants.

   and   which   particularly

   _____

   _____

A Rewrite the story in six sentences on your own lined paper.

A boy and his cat were sitting on the porch. The cat looked content, but it was unhappy. It wanted to catch mice and chase after birds.

B

eyes   emeralds

1. Tell how the objects could be the same.

_____

_____

2. Write a simile about the objects.

_____

_____

C Answer the questions.

1. What's the rule about when the demand is less than the supply?

_____

_____

_____

2. What's the rule about when the demand is greater than the supply?

_____

_____

_____

3. What's the rule about what manufacturers try to do?

_____

_____

_____

Pete's Shoe Store can't sell all its shoes.

4. Which is greater, the supply or the demand?

_____

5. What will happen to the price of shoes?

_____

How do you know?

_____

_____

In the spring, Pete's Shoe Store lowers its prices on boots.

7. Which is greater, the supply or the demand?

_____

8. How do you know?

_____

_____

9. What will the boot manufacturer try to do?

_____

_____

Name two ways that the manufacturers can do that.

10. _____

11. _____

 For each sentence followed by a blank, write in the number of the rule that relates to that sentence.

1. **When the demand is greater than the supply, prices go up.**
2. **When the demand is less than the supply, prices go down.**

The demand for gas is always growing. When there is a surplus of gas, consumers are happy because their bills are low. _____ But when there is a shortage of gas, consumers' wallets are hit hard. _____ Some dishonest companies have tried to create fake shortages. They have made consumers believe that there is almost no gas left, which means that prices will have to change. _____ When the price gets up to where they want it, they "find" more gas and sell it for the new price. This is a pretty slick con game, and it is against the law.

E Underline the redundant sentences.

The zoo owned a giant ape named Gog. Gog was so big that he could jump over houses and lift cars with one hand. One day, Gog broke out of his cage and started walking around town, crushing mailboxes and fire hydrants with his feet. Gog belonged to the zoo. He saw men loading bananas onto a truck and he roared with joy. The men ran away. Gog wasn't very small, and he could lift men with a single hand. He grabbed six hundred bananas and took them back to his cage. His cage was broken.

F Use the rule to answer the questions.

The hotter the liquid, the faster it evaporates.

1. The water in the cup is eighty degrees.
The water in the glass is fifty degrees.
a. Which water is hotter?

_____

b. Which water will evaporate faster?

_____

c. How do you know?

_____

_____

2. Gene's soda pop evaporated in thirty minutes.
Lin's soda pop evaporated in sixty minutes.
a. Whose soda pop evaporated faster?

_____

b. Whose soda pop was hotter?

_____

c. How do you know?

_____

_____

G Fill in each blank with the word that has the same meaning as the word or words under the blank.

1. The basketball player _____
   (changed)
her shot.

2. The play has a very strange _____.
   (end)

3. Companies do not _____
   (make in a factory)
live trees.

4. A good swimmer can _____
   (breathe)
very slowly.

H Cross out the wrong word and write the correct word above it. **(4)**

Last year, Mr. Jeter decided to modify his house because his house were too small. He wanted to build an extra bedroom and a family room. Mr. Jeter had tools, but he have no wood. She went to the lumber yard and bought some pine. When Mr. Jeter are building the extra rooms, he hit his hand with the hammer. Mr. Jeter yelled so loudly that all his neighbors heard him.

I Fill in each blank.

1. _____

2. _____

3. _____

4. _____

5. _____

6. _____

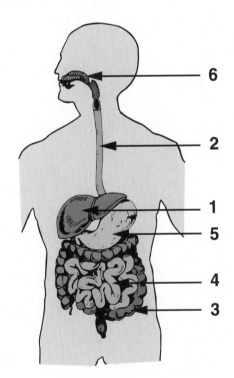

J Read the story and answer the questions. Circle the **W** if the question is answered by words in the story, and underline those words. Circle the **D** if the question is answered by a deduction.

Here's another rule about demand and supply: Manufacturers try to make the demand greater than the supply. Mr. Franklin runs the only lightbulb factory in Mudville. In May, he produces just as many lightbulbs as Mudville needs, which is 1000 a month. Mr. Franklin makes 50¢ for each lightbulb he sells that month. In June, Mr. Franklin decides that he wants to make more than 50¢ for each lightbulb he sells. He knows that if he can make the demand greater than the supply, the price of lightbulbs will go up. So he puts an ad in the paper that says, "If you have more lights in your house, you will be able to see your house better. You won't stub your toes in dark corners, you will be able to read anywhere, and your house will be cheery." The ad works, and the demand for lightbulbs goes up. Because the demand is so high, Mr. Franklin raises the price of his lightbulbs, and he sells all 1000 of them.

1. What's another rule about demand and supply?

   _____

   _____

   _____

2. How much money did Mr. Franklin make in May?

   _____ **W**   **D**

3. What did the ad try to make people think?

   _____

   _____ **W**   **D**

4. Why is Mr. Franklin able to sell all 1000 of his light bulbs in June at the higher price?

   _____

   _____ **W**   **D**

5. Name another way that Mr. Franklin could have increased the demand.

   _____

   _____

6. What would happen to the demand if the ad did not work?

   _____

   _____ **W**   **D**

7. If Mr. Franklin makes 60¢ for each light bulb he sells in June, how much money will he make that month?

   _____

 Follow the directions.

1. Draw a horizontal line.
2. Draw a line that slants down to the left from the left end of the horizontal line.
3. At the bottom of the slanted line, draw an arrow that points down to the right.
4. Draw the muscle that will move the slanted line in the direction of the arrow.

A Read the story and answer the questions. Circle the **W** if the question is answered by words in the story, and underline those words. Circle the **D** if the question is answered by a deduction.

> Mrs. Jenkins runs the only flour mill in Zork City. In October, her mill produces only 1000 pounds, which is half as much flour as Zork City needs each month. Because the demand is so much greater than the supply, she charges $1 a pound for her flour. Mr. Ross thinks that he can make money if he starts another flour mill in Zork City that will compete with Mrs. Jenkins's mill. In November, he puts 1500 pounds up for sale at 75¢ a pound. Everybody starts buying Mr. Ross's flour. Then Mrs. Jenkins, who needs to sell her flour, lowers her price to 50¢ a pound. Everybody starts buying Mrs. Jenkins's flour again. Each mill keeps lowering the price of flour until the price is as low as it can be. This is called a price war, and it always makes consumers very happy.

1. Why can Mrs. Jenkins charge so much for flour in October?

_____

_____

_____ W   D

2. Which was greater in November, the supply or the demand?

_____ W   D

3. Why did Mr. Ross sell his flour for less than Mrs. Jenkins's flour?

_____

_____ W   D

4. What did Mr. Ross do after Mrs. Jenkins lowered her price to 50¢?

_____

_____

5. Flour prices went down in November because of the price war. Give another reason why they went down.

_____

_____ W   D

6. If both mills end up charging 40¢ a pound for flour, how can one mill attract more customers?

_____

_____

7. Why do price wars make consumers happy?

_____

_____ W   D

B Rewrite the story in six sentences on your own lined paper.

Samuel Clemens, who is better known as Mark Twain, was one of the greatest writers in American history. Although he is best known for his sense of humor, he wrote many serious works. As he grew older, Twain became bitter about many things, particularly American morality.

C Underline the redundant sentences.

When Gog got back to his cage, the zookeeper was having a fit. He took away Gog's bananas and made him fix the cage. Gog was sad. Gog did what the zookeeper told him to do. The zookeeper was really mad at Gog. He said, "You're lucky you didn't kill anybody today. If you had, we would have had to send you to the big banana in the sky." Gog was not happy. His cage was a mess, but the town was worse. Water was everywhere, and letters blew about like leaves in the wind. Happily, nobody was dead.

D Label each nerve. Write a message for each nerve.

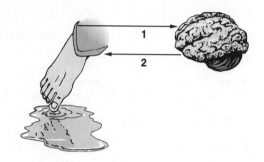

1. _____

2. _____

 E

words   knives

1. Tell how the objects could be the same.

_____

_____

2. Write a simile about the objects.

_____

_____

skin   milk

3. Tell how the objects could be the same.

_____

_____

4. Write a simile about the objects.

_____

_____

F Make each statement mean the same thing as the statement in the box.

> **Although every person produces carbon dioxide, there is not much in the air.**

1. All people produce carbon dioxide, but there is not much in the air.
2. Although people use up carbon dioxide, there isn't a lot in the air.
3. Every person makes carbon dioxide, but there's a lot in the air.
4. Although there is not much carbon dioxide in the air, every person consumes it.

G Write the middle part of each deduction.

1. Some storms generate electricity.

   _____

   So, maybe tornados generate electricity.
2. Steve had some Mexican coins.

   _____

   So, maybe Steve had a peso.
3. Some lakes have salt water.

   _____

   So, maybe Lake Erie has salt water.

H Answer the questions.

1. What's the rule about when the demand is greater than the supply?

   _____

   _____

   _____

2. What's the rule about when the demand is less than the supply?

   _____

   _____

   _____

> **Twenty people want to buy swimming pools. Jan's Sporting Goods has thirty swimming pools.**

3. Which is greater, the supply or the demand?

   _____

4. What will happen to the price of swimming pools?

   _____

5. How do you know?

   _____

   _____

6. What will the manufacturers try to do?

   _____

   _____

**Name two ways that the
manufacturers can do that.**

7. _____

8. _____

**In the summer, the price of
swimming pools goes up.**

9. Which is greater, the supply or the demand?

_____

10. How do you know?

_____

_____

I For each sentence followed by a blank,
write in the number of the rule that
relates to that sentence.

1. **Like magnetic poles repel one
another.**
2. **Unlike magnetic poles attract one
another.**

Many years ago, a magician amazed people
with a "floating-magnet" trick. He used two ring
magnets and a stick. Holding the stick up in one
hand, he would slide the first ring down the
stick with the north pole facing up. Then he
would slide the second ring down the stick with
the north pole facing down. The second ring
wouldn't touch the first ring. _____ It
"floated" above the first ring. _____ Then
the magician would slide the top ring off, turn it
around, and slide it back down the stick. This
time, the two rings stuck together like

glue. _____ When he slid the top ring up,
the bottom ring came with it. _____ This
trick is easy to understand now, but it took
people a long time to figure it out.

J Write a word that comes from **construct**
or **consume** in each blank. Then write
verb, noun, or **adjective** after each item.

1. We need to _____ less
gasoline. _____

2. Some _____ costs billions of
dollars. _____

3. _____ should know more about
supply and demand. _____

4. That town was not _____ ten
years ago. _____

5. Food is _____, so people
must buy it all the time. _____

K Follow the directions.

1. Draw a circle.
2. Draw a horizontal line from the left side of
the circle to the right side of the circle.
3. Above the line, write the word that means
that something involves participation.
4. Below the line, write what part of speech that
word is.

A Rewrite the story in six sentences on your own lined paper.

One of the rarest bills in the world is the American $10,000 bill, which was last made in 1944. The bill pictures Salmon P. Chase, who was a nineteenth-century judge. A few banks still have some of these bills, but they never use them.

B Combine the sentences with **however.**

1. John made his selection.
   John didn't get what he wanted.

   _____

   _____

   _____

2. Frogs are born in the water.
   Frogs grow up on the land.

   _____

   _____

   _____

3. He modified the car.
   The car looked the same.

   _____

   _____

   _____

4. Bats are not birds.
   Bats fly.

   _____

   _____

   _____

C Underline the redundant sentences.

The man went from house to house, trying to get people to buy brushes. He was not having very good luck. The man was a salesman. The man had a standard sales pitch. He told people that their lives would change if they bought his brushes. Not many people fell for this pitch. The man decided to modify his sales pitch. When he tried to sell his brushes, he gave people a different pitch.

D Write a word that comes from **erode** in each blank. Then write **verb, noun,** or **adjective** after each item.

1. Farmers are learning to prevent soil

   _____. _____

2. Water has a lot of _____

   power. _____

3. The sea will _____ its

   shoreline. _____

4. Wind has _____ rocks in the

desire. _____

5. Rain is a very _____ force.

_____

E Read the story and answer the questions. Circle the **W** if the question is answered by words in the story, and underline those words. Circle the **D** if the question is answered by a deduction.

> Mr. Bock runs the only pen factory in Zork City. Mr. Bock makes his pens very cheaply, and they are not very good. But he can still sell them because the demand is so high. However, Mrs. Flap starts another pen factory in Zork City. Her pens are better made, and they cost the same as Mr. Bock's. Pretty soon, everybody is buying Mrs. Flap's pens. Mr. Bock has to make his pens even better than Mrs. Flap's. People start buying his pens again. Each factory keeps improving its pens until the pens are of top quality. The people of Zork City are very happy, except for Mr. Bock, who liked the early days better.

1. Why weren't Mr. Bock's pens very good?

_____

_____

2. Why did people in Zork City buy his pens?

_____

_____

3. Why did Mrs. Flap make her pens better than Mr. Bock's pens?

_____

_____

_____ **W**   **D**

4. What might have happened to Mr. Bock if he had kept on making the same old pens?

_____

_____ **W**   **D**

5. Car manufacturers always compete with each other. Here are some ways that cars have improved because of competition: better gas mileage, more legroom, disk brakes. Name three more.

_____

_____

_____

6. Name another manufactured product that has improved because of competition.

_____

7. How has it improved?

_____

_____

F For each sentence followed by a blank, write in the number of the rule that relates to that sentence.

> 1. **When the demand is less than the supply, prices go down.**
> 2. **Manufacturers try to make the demand greater than the supply.**

It was a dry winter, and there was no snow on the mountains. The ski factory was losing a lot of money. _____ The factory owner tried to get the ski resorts to buy a snow-making machine. _____ He said, "If we don't get snow on the slopes soon, we'll all go out of business. _____ We need to put lots of ads on TV to show that machine-made snow is just as good as the real thing." _____ So they did. People tried the new snow, but they did not like it. The ski manufacturer was glad when the winter was over. It had been a very bad year for his company, and he had almost gone broke. _____

G Tell which fact each statement relates to. Make each contradiction true.

> 1. **The demand for gas is greater than the supply of gas.**
> 2. **The gas company is trying to make the demand even bigger.**

a. The gas company put an ad on TV that told people to use less gas. _____

b. The price kept going down. _____

c. They want to make more money. _____

H Write the instructions.

1. _____

   _____

2. _____

   _____

   _____

3. _____

   _____

   _____

I Answer the questions.

1. What's the rule about when the demand is less than the supply?

   _____

   _____

   _____

2. What's the rule about what manufacturers try to do?

   _____

   _____

   _____

Lin's Bakery has 40 loaves of bread.

50 people want loaves of bread.

3. Which is greater, the supply or the demand?

_____

4. What will happen to the price of bread?

_____

5. How do you know?

_____

_____

Last week, a loaf of bread cost 50¢.

This week, a loaf of bread costs 40¢.

6. What happened to the price of bread?

_____

7. Which was greater, the supply or the demand?

_____

8. What will the manufacturers try to do?

_____

_____

Name two ways that the

manufacturers can do that.

9. _____

10. _____

_____

J Make up a simile for each item.

1. That football player runs right over everyone.

_____

_____

2. His fingers are long and thin.

_____

_____

K Write the conclusion of each deduction.

1. Some minerals help your body.
   Iron is a mineral.

_____

_____

2. Some body cells are long and thin.
   Bone cells are body cells.

_____

_____

3. Tom has every kind of tooth.
   A molar is a tooth.

_____

_____

WORD LIST

Central nervous system (n) *means* the body system that is made up of the brain and spinal cord.

Circulate (v) *means* move around.

Conclude (v) *means* end or figure out.

Conclusive (a) *means* that something is true without any doubt.

Manufacturer (n) *means* something that manufactures.

Nervous system (n) *means* the body system of nerves.

Peripheral nervous system (n) *means* the body system that is made up of all the nerves that lead to and from the spinal cord.

Protection (n) *means* something that protects.

Regulation (n) *means* a rule.

Residence (n) *means* a place where someone resides.

Residential (a) *means* that a place has many residences.

Respire (v) *means* breathe.

Selection (n) *means* something that is selected.

Simile (n) *means* a statement that tells how things are the same.

ERRORS	O	W	B	T

A — Combine the sentences with **however.**

1. She ate a big lunch.
She still felt hungry.

_____

_____

2. Mike went to the store.
Mike didn't buy anything.

_____

_____

3. Pat has a broken femur.
Pat can walk fast.

_____

_____

4. That woman makes many criticisms.
That woman is very kind.

_____

_____

_____

B — Cross out the wrong word and write the correct word above it.   (4)

My dog is a bulldog. Many people is
afraid of bulldogs, but my dog is a very
nice dog. We goes walking every day in
the park. I keep him tied in the backyard,
but sometimes he get loose. If you ever see
a bulldog with a green collar, that's my
dog. Her name is Sam.

C — Underline the contradiction. Circle the statement it contradicts. Tell **why** the underlined statement contradicts the circled statement. Make the underlined statement true.

The Popper Company was a large
toaster manufacturer. Most of the people in
Popsville worked for the Popper Company.
Joyce worked for the advertising
department, and she liked her job. Every
day, she participated in basketball games
at the factory. * Besides taking part in
basketball games, Joyce predicted what
kinds of toasters people wanted. The
Popper Company always tried to make
people want fewer toasters than it could
make. Joyce was very good at writing ads
for the toasters.

_____

_____

_____

D Make up a simile for each item.

1. Her skin was tough and wrinkled.

_____

_____

2. His eyes were very bright.

_____

_____

E Use the facts to fill out the form.

Facts: Your name is Otis Buckley. You have never had a job. You live with your parents. Your address is 122 Oakway, Charlotte, NC. You graduated from high school last year. You had a C average in school. Your favorite class was art. Your art teacher, Mr. Collins, thought you were very talented. You are applying for a job as a window decorator in a department store.

Instructions:
  a. Print your name on line 2.
  b. Print the name of your current employer on line 3.
  c. On line 1, write the highest grade you have completed in school.
  d. Print your address on line 5.
  e. On line 4, list any experience you have had in this position **or** reasons why you feel qualified for this position.
  f. On line 6, give the name of a person who could recommend you for this position.

  g. Cross out the second sentence that gives information you didn't use.

1. _____

2. _____

3. _____

4. _____

_____

5. _____

_____

6. _____

F Rewrite the story in six sentences on your own lined paper.

North and South America have many baseball teams. People on both continents love to go to baseball games, particularly on the weekends. Baseball will always have fans because it is so much fun to watch.

G Write a word that comes from **erode** in each blank. Then write **verb, noun,** or **adjective** after each item.

1. The earth loses a lot of productive land

   through _____. _____

2. We can't afford to let good cropland be

   _____. _____

3. Wind and water are _____

   forces. _____

4. Rain can swell rivers and _____

   their banks. _____

5. Wind can _____ land in hot,

   dry weather. _____

H Underline the redundant sentences.

Jeff looked at the catcher's mitt, waiting for the signal. The batter looked like she could really hit, and Jeff was worried. The catcher signaled a fastball. Jeff got ready to throw. He was a pitcher, and he was playing a game. He threw the ball fast. The batter seemed to have the strength to really whack the ball. She swung hard, but the ball whizzed by her. Jeff had thrown a strike. The crowd cheered.

I Write the instructions.

② erode   ①

③

1. _____

2. _____

   _____

3. _____

   _____

A Combine the sentences with **however.**

1. He likes participatory sports.
   He doesn't like basketball.

   _____

   _____

   _____

2. Ted was very happy.
   Ted was frowning.

   _____

   _____

3. Smoking is bad for people's lungs.
   Many people like smoking.

   _____

   _____

   _____

4. She is very productive.
   She has always been lazy.

   _____

   _____

B Answer the questions.

1. What's the rule about products that are
   readier to use?

   _____

   _____

2. Which is readier to use, a cake or a cake
   mix?

   _____

3. So, what else do you know about a cake?

   _____

4. How do you know?

   _____

5. Which costs more, a bike that's put together
   or a bike that comes in parts?

   _____

6. How do you know?

   _____

   > **Mr. Marek gets chicken in a**
   > **restaurant.**
   > **Mr. Montini gets raw chicken in a**
   > **store and then spends an hour**
   > **cooking it.**

7. Whose chicken costs more?

   _____

8. How do you know?

   _____

   _____

C

man	**gorilla**

1. Tell how the objects could be the same.

_____

_____

2. Write a simile about the objects.

_____

_____

D Underline the contradiction. Circle the statement it contradicts. Tell **why** the underlined statement contradicts the circled statement. Make the underlined statement true.

Before Nelly opened her new dress shop, she put an ad in the paper. Customers filled the shop soon after it opened. They wanted more dresses than Nelly had. * Nelly was very happy. She lowered her prices. Then she called the paper and told them to run the ad for another week.

_____

_____

E Write a word that comes from **produce** or **circulate** in each blank. Then write **verb, noun,** or **adjective** after each item.

1. Smoking may hurt the _____ in your legs. _____

2. Many things are _____ by machines. _____

3. Our crop _____ went down last year. _____

4. She wants to be a more _____ writer. _____

5. Food sellers often _____ at ball games. _____

F Cross out the wrong word and write the correct word above it.   **(4)**

Many people don't like their jobs, but most fire fighters is happy with their work. A fire fighter's job is a popular job. Most cities has a long list of people waiting to be fire fighters. If you are hired as a fire fighter, you must spent several months training for the job. You must run, exercise, and climb ropes and ladders. Fire fighters mustn't be very strong, because their work is very hard.

G Rewrite the paragraph in four sentences on your ownlined paper. If one of the sentences tells **why,** combine the sentences with **because.** If sentences seem contradictory, combine them with **although.**

Much of the music you hear comes from jazz. Jazz was invented in the United States. Jazz started with black slaves. Black slaves came from Africa. They sang to keep their spirits up. They led very hard lives. Their first songs were almost all African. Their later songs began to change.

H Underline the redundant sentences.

Pete dribbled the ball down the court. He looked at the scoreboard. Only three seconds were left. Pete was playing basketball. His team had seventy-five points, but the other team had seventy-six points. There was less than one minute to play. Pete's team was behind. Pete shot the ball. It circled the rim twice and finally dropped in. Pete's team started cheering. Pete had made the basket. His team had won by one point.

I Use the facts to fill out the form.

Facts: Your name is Virgil Johnson. You have lived at 112 Bingham Lane in Salem, Oregon, for three years. Your rent is $350 a month, and your car payments are $200 a month. You were born February 2, 1975. Your first job, which you started in 1993, was with American Title Company. Since 1995, you have worked for Juniper Credit, and you make $1800 a month. You have no credit cards, and you are divorced. You are filling out a credit application to obtain a stereo.

Instructions:
1. Name, last name first:

   _____

2. Age: _____
3. Most recent employer:

   _____

4. How long have you worked there?

   _____

5. Are you married? _____
6. Monthly income: _____
7. Total monthly rent and car payments:

   _____

8. Address: _____

   _____

Rewrite the story in six sentences on your own lined paper.

Hard balls and wooden bats were used in other sports before baseball. Americans, who love sports, invented a game that made use of hard balls and wooden bats in the 1840s. Although the game was complex, it was soon being played by many people.

  Follow the directions.

1. Draw a vertical line.
2. Draw another vertical line to the right of the first line.
3. Draw a horizontal line from the bottom of the first line to the bottom of the second line.
4. Between the vertical lines, write the word that means **how well something sells.**

A Answer the questions.

1. What's the rule about products that are readier to use?

_____

_____

2. Which is readier to use, a ready-made skirt or material and a pattern?

_____

3. So, what else do you know about a ready-made skirt?

_____

4. How do you know?

_____

_____

5. Which costs more, a model that you have to put together or a model that is already put together?

_____

_____

6. How do you know?

_____

_____

> **Mrs. Anderson obtains 5 pounds of frozen French fries.**
> **Mrs. Miller obtains 5 pounds of cooked French fries.**

7. Whose French fries cost more?

_____

8. How do you know?

_____

_____

B Combine the sentences with **however.**

1. The man modified his car.
His car still did not run.

_____

_____

2. Vern hurt his quadriceps.
Vern won the race.

_____

_____

3. They had a big supply of tennis shoes.
They ran out.

_____

_____

_____

4. She concluded her speech.
She kept on talking.

_____

_____

C Underline the redundant sentences. Circle and correct the punctuation errors.

A bell rang. Sam put on his fire fighter's hat and his fire fighter's coat He jumped on the fire truck as it roared out of the station. Sam was a fire fighter. The truck sped down Oak Street and screeched around the corner of Oak and First. The truck was going sixty miles an hour however it could have gone a lot faster. The truck was speeding along. The truck screamed to a stop at First and Elm. Sam jumped off to look for a fire hydrant which wasn't easy. The fire was at First and Elm.

D Underline the nouns. Draw a line **over** the adjectives. Circle the verbs.

1. Wind and water were eroding the mountain.

2. That stream has eroded its banks.

3. A large black goat was under a tree.

4. Erosion changes everything on the planet.

E Draw in the arrows. Tell if each tube is a vein or an artery. Tell what gas each tube carries.

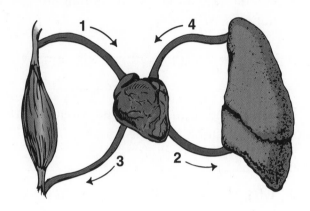

1. _____

2. _____

3. _____

4. _____

F Write a word that comes from **obtain** or **respire** in each blank. Then write **verb, noun,** or **adjective** after each item.

1. She is trying to _____ new tires. _____

2. After you run, your _____ is much faster. _____

3. Your bronchial tubes are in your _____ system. _____

4. That country is _____ new jets. _____

5. You should _____ slowly if you feel dizzy. _____

voice   gravel

1. Tell how the objects could be the same.

_____

_____

2. Write a simile about the objects.

_____

_____

lips   cherries

3. Tell how the objects could be the same.

_____

_____

4. Write a simile about the objects.

_____

_____

H Read the story and answer the questions. Circle the **W** if the question is answered by words in the story, and underline those words. Circle the **D** if the question is answered by a deduction.

Here's another rule about demand and supply: When the demand is less than the supply, prices go down. Mrs. Thomas runs the only dairy farm near Newton. In July, her cows produce just as much milk as Newton needs, which is 1000 gallons a month. In August, a big group of people moves out of Newton, and Newton's demand for milk drops to 600 gallons a month. But Mrs. Thomas's cows are still producing 1000 gallons a month. She sells 600 gallons at the old price, and then she is stuck with 400 gallons that will soon go bad. Mrs. Thomas thinks that she can get people to buy the 400 gallons if she lowers the price. Her idea works, and she sells all 400 gallons at the lower price.

1. What's the rule?

_____

_____

_____

2. What would have happened to the price of milk if a big group of people had moved into Newton in July?

_____

_____ **W**   **D**

3. Was the demand smaller than the supply in August because the demand went down or because the supply went up?

_____

_____

4. What does Mrs. Thomas do to get people to buy the 400 gallons she had left over?

_____ **W**   **D**

5. What does Mrs. Thomas have to do to the demand to sell 1000 gallons at the old price in September?

_____

_____ **W**   **D**

6. Name one way she could do that.

_____

_____

7. Did Mrs. Thomas lose money in August?

_____ **W**   **D**

[I] Rewrite the story in six sentences on your own lined paper.

> Many great players played for the Los Angeles Dodgers, particularly in the 1960s. One very famous player was Sandy Koufax, who was an amazing pitcher. His style and speed are copied by many pitchers today.

[J] Rewrite the paragraph in four sentences on your own lined paper. If one of the sentences tells **why,** combine the sentences with **because.** If sentences seem contradictory, combine them with **although.**

> The singers sang many kinds of songs. The singers sang mostly work songs and love songs. Most of their music was sung without instruments. Some of their music was sung with instruments. The singers started singing together in 1995. 1995 is when they finished high school. Sometimes, the singers perform in churches. Churches are all over town.

 Follow the directions.

1. Draw a horizontal line.
2. Draw a line that slants down to the right from the right end of the horizontal line.
3. At the bottom of the slanted line, draw an arrow that points down to the left.
4. Draw the muscle that will move the slanted line in the direction of the arrow.

A Underline the redundant sentences.
Circle and correct the punctuation errors.

Mr. Alper had a problem. He had ordered a big, supply of sandals in August. Now it was October, and nobody was buying sandals. Mr. Alper started advertising his sandals, but nobody bought them. Advertising didn't work. So Mr. Alper decided to have a big sale. He put a sign on his door; that said, "Two pairs of sandals for the price of one." His store started to fill with customers. Customers were all over his store. Although he sold many sandals he still had some left after the sale.

B Answer the questions.

1. What's the rule about products that are readier to use?

_____

_____

2. Which is readier to use, a car that needs repairs or a car that runs perfectly?

_____

_____

3. So, what else do you know about that car?

_____

4. How do you know?

_____

Frozen fish costs less than cooked fish.

5. Which is readier to use when you obtain it?

_____

6. How do you know?

_____

Andrew and Mike shop at the same store. On Thursday, they both have meat pie for dinner. Andrew's pie costs 50¢. Mike's pie costs $2.

7. Whose dinner was readier to eat when he obtained it?

_____

8. Who spent more time fixing dinner?

_____

C Circle the word that combines the sentences correctly. Combine the sentences with that word.

1. Those striking workers are circulating leaflets.
   Those striking workers are giving speeches.
   however   which   and

   _____

   _____

   _____

2. Mary is always late.
   Mary will lose her job.
   however   particularly   because

   _____

   _____

3. That person is lazy.
   That person is productive.
   who   but   because

   _____

   _____

4. The monkey is consuming carrots.
   A gorilla is consuming carrots.
   and   however   because

   _____

   _____

5. The man manufactured spoons.
   Spoons were in low demand.
   because   however   which

   _____

   _____

D Write what each analogy tells.

What part of speech each word is
What verb each word comes from
What each word means
What ending each word has

1. **Erosion** is to **ion** as **respiratory** is to **ory.**

   _____

   _____

2. **Erosion** is to **noun** as **respiratory** is to **adjective.**

   _____

   _____

3. **Erosion** is to **erode** as **respiratory** is to **respire.**

   _____

   _____

E Fill in each blank.

1. _____

2. _____

3. _____

4. _____

5. _____

6. _____

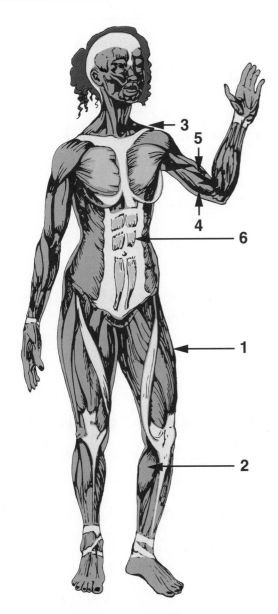

F Read the story and answer the questions. Circle the **W** if the question is answered by words in the story, and underline those words. Circle the **D** if the question is answered by a deduction.

You know that when the demand is less than the supply, prices go down. Mr. Hightower runs the only chicken farm near Newton. In September, his chickens produce just as many eggs as Newton needs, which is 1000 dozen a month. Mr. Hightower sells the eggs for $2 a dozen, so he makes $2000 that month. The people of Newton think that $2 a dozen is too much to pay for eggs. In October, they all get together and decide not to buy eggs from Mr. Hightower. This is called a boycott. Mr. Hightower, whose chickens are still producing eggs, is stuck with 1000 dozen eggs that will soon go bad. The only way he can make any money in October is to lower the price of eggs and to hope that people will like the new price. So he lowers the price to $1 a dozen. The people of Newton like this new price, and they buy all the eggs.

1. What's the rule?

_____

_____

_____

2. Why do people decide not to buy eggs in October?

_____

_____

_____

3. Why was Mr. Hightower stuck with 1000 dozen eggs?

_____

_____ W   D

4. Was the demand smaller than the supply because the demand went down or because the supply went up?

_____

_____ W   D

5. Why did Mr. Hightower lower the price?

_____

_____

6. How much did Mr. Hightower make in October?

_____

7. What does a boycott do to the demand?

_____ W   D

G Circle the subject and underline the predicate. Rewrite each sentence by moving part of the predicate.

1. Hank played tennis while the sun was out.

_____

_____

2. The weather was very dry last winter.

_____

_____

3. Many people ride bikes in China.

_____

_____

4. You must have a license to drive a car.

_____

_____

H Answer the questions.

1. What's the rule about when the demand is greater than the supply?

_____

_____

After a mild winter, the demand for lemons is less than the supply of lemons.

2. What will happen to the price of lemons?

_____

3. How do you know?

_____

_____

4. What will the farmers try to do?

_____

_____

Name two ways that the farmers can do that.

5. _____

6. _____

After a bad winter, the demand for lemons is greater than the supply of lemons.

7. What will happen to the price of lemons?

_____

8. How do you know?

_____

_____

Last winter, lemons cost 89¢ a pound.
This winter, lemons cost 39¢ a pound.

9. What happened to the price of lemons?

_____

10. Which was greater, the supply or the demand?

_____

I Rewrite the story in six sentences on your own lined paper.

Babe Ruth could really hit the ball; however, he could not run very fast. For many years, he held the home-run record and the total hit record. His hat and glove are kept in the Baseball Hall of Fame.

J Write **R** for each fact that is **relevant** to what happened. Write **I** for each fact that is **irrelevant** to what happened.

Mrs. Nelson buys raw meat because it costs less than cooked meat.

1. Mrs. Nelson wants to save money. _____

2. Mrs. Nelson goes shopping on Saturdays. _____

3. Mrs. Nelson can speak Spanish. _____

4. Mrs. Nelson doesn't have much money. _____

A Answer the questions.

1. What's the rule about products that are readier to use?

_____

_____

2. Which is readier to use, a balloon with air in it or a balloon without any air in it?

_____

_____

3. So, what else do you know about that balloon?

_____

4. How do you know?

_____

> **Bob acquires a model plane and spends two months putting it together. Tom obtains a model plane at the store and plays with it that night.**

5. Whose model plane cost more? _____

6. How do you know?

_____

7. If you want to save money, is it better to buy cooked meat or raw meat?

_____

8. If you want to save time, is it better to buy cooked meat or raw meat?

_____

B Put the statements below the story in the right order.

> Before Bill made a kite, he got a book on kite building and studied it for a long time. The first kite Bill constructed was a Chinese snake kite. It had a tail that was ten meters long. The tail got tangled up in a tree, and Bill lost the kite. So he made a box kite. It was the highest-flying kite he made. It went up over two thousand meters. Sadly, the string broke and Bill never found the kite. The last kite Bill made was a diving kite. He could make it dive by letting the string go slack. To pull the kite out of a dive, Bill pulled hard on the string.

He made a kite that went very high. _____

He made a snake kite. _____

He made a diving kite. _____

He got a book. _____

A kite got stuck in a tree. _____

He studied a book. _____

C Write a word that comes from **acquire** in each blank. Then write **verb, noun,** or **adjective** after each item.

1. Art collectors are _____.

_____

2. He _____ some tools to

construct a shed. _____

3. Rosa is _____ a lot of

money. _____

4. His coat is an expensive _____.

_____

5. Many rich people are very _____.

_____

D Complete the analogies.

1. Tell what part of speech each word is.

Participatory is to _____

as **circulation** is to _____.

2. Tell what verb each word comes from.

Participatory is to _____

as **circulatory** is to _____.

3. Tell what each word means.

Participatory is to _____

_____

as **circulation** is to _____

_____.

E Draw the arrow for each nerve. Write a message for each nerve.

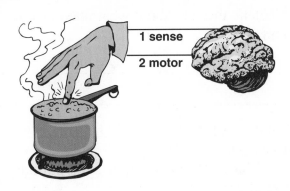

1. _____

2. _____

F Underline the redundant sentences. Circle and correct the punctuation errors.

Sally got hit with a baseball, bat in her arm. Her humerus was cracked. When she was injured, the bone in her upper arm was broken. Sally went to a doctor The doctor told Sally that she would have to wear a cast however Sally did not want to wear one. The doctor told Sally that she had no choice. There was nothing else that Sally could do. So the doctor put the cast on Sally's arm, It was so heavy that Sally needed a sling around her neck to hold it up

G Answer the questions.

1. What's the rule about what manufacturers try to do?

_____

_____

_____

> **Mike's Dairy produces 100 pounds of butter a week.**
>
> **Mike's Dairy sells 70 pounds of butter a week.**

2. Which is greater, the supply or the demand?

_____

3. What will happen to the price of butter?

_____

4. How do you know?

_____

_____

5. What will Mike's Dairy try to do?

_____

_____

> **Name two ways that Mike's Dairy can do that.**

6. _____

_____

7. _____

> **Last week, the price of cheese at Mike's Dairy went down.**

8. Which was greater, the supply or the demand?

_____

9. How do you know?

_____

_____

> **Today, the price of milk at Mike's Dairy went up.**

10. Which was greater, the supply or the demand?

_____

H Make each statement mean the same thing as the statement in the box.

> **Ron was very shy; however, he always participated in class.**

1. Although Ron was very shy, he never took part in class.

2. Ron always took part in class, but he was very shy.

3. Ron was very shy, but he never took part in class.

4. Ron, who was very shy, always participated in class.

I Write the conclusion of each deduction.

1. Some rock comes from volcanoes.
Granite is rock.

_____

_____

2. Burning things produce carbon dioxide.
Fires are burning things.

_____

_____

3. All oceans are made up of salt water.
The Pacific is an ocean.

_____

_____

J Circle the word that combines the sentences correctly. Combine the sentences with that word.

1. The femurs support the pelvis.

The femurs are the longest bones in the body.

who   which   because

_____

_____

_____

2. That woman has swum across the lake.

Her children have swum across the lake.

although   and   because

_____

_____

_____

3. Her older brother modifies cars.

My dad modifies cars.

who   although   and

_____

_____

4. Wind was eroding the mountain.

Rain was eroding the mountain.

which   however   and

_____

_____

5. The fat cat is hungry.

The fat cat won't eat.

because   however   particularly

_____

_____

Rewrite the story in eight sentences on your own lined paper.

Roger Maris, who played for the New York Yankees, broke Babe Ruth's single-season home-run record by hitting 61 home runs in one season. Maris's record looked unbeatable; however, it was broken in 1998 by two players. One player was Sammy Sosa, who hit 66 home runs. The other player was Mark McGwire, who hit 70 home runs.

WORD LIST

Brain (n) *means* the organ that lets you think and feel.

Constructive (a) *means* that something is helpful.

Consume (v) *means* **use up or eat.**

Erode (v) *means* wear things down.

Erosion (n) *means* what happens when something is eroded.

Erosive (a) *means* that something erodes.

Examine (v) *means* look at.

Heart (n) *means* the pump that moves the blood.

Modification (n) *means* a change.

Nerve (n) *means* a wire in the body that carries messages.

Obtain (v) *means* get.

Participate (v) *means* take part in something.

Predictable (a) *means* that something is easy to predict.

Spinal cord (n) *means* the body part that connects the brain to all parts of the body.

A Put the statements below the story in the right order.

> **Susan got up early in the morning on Saturday and washed her hair. She made coffee and woke up her roommate. "Get up," she said. "It's a sunny day!" Her roommate got up and they drank coffee together. Then Susan's roommate went off to play golf. Susan dried her hair in the sun and pulled weeds from her garden. Then she went into the house and watered her plants. "I need to obtain new pots for some of these plants," Susan said to herself. So she went to the store. When Susan came home again, her roommate was back from golf. They made a big salad and ate it outside in the warm sun.**

She said, "It's a sunny day!" _____

She watered her plants. _____

She woke up early in the morning. _____

Her roommate went off to play golf. _____

She dried her hair. _____

She went to the store. _____

B Write the instructions.

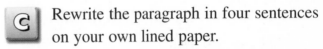

① _____

acquisition

③ _____

②

1. _____

_____

2. _____

_____

3. _____

_____

C Rewrite the paragraph in four sentences on your own lined paper.

a. If one of the sentences tells **why,** combine the sentences with **because.**

b. If two sentences seem contradictory, combine them with **however.**

c. Move part of the predicate in sentences that you don't combine.

> Many black jazz musicians started getting famous around 1900. Scott Joplin became very popular for his style of jazz piano. His style of jazz piano was called ragtime. Joplin did not live very long. Joplin wrote many songs. Ragtime piano was played all over the country in only a few years.

D Answer the questions.

1. What's the rule about products that are readier to use?

_____

_____

2. Which costs more, a table that is ready to use or a table that comes in parts?

_____

_____

3. How do you know?

_____

> **Linda and Sally are wearing the same kind of dress. Linda's was already made when she acquired it. Sally made her dress herself.**

4. Whose dress cost more?

_____

5. How do you know?

_____

> **Tom and Rob shop at the same store. On Friday, they both have a glass of lemonade. Tom's lemonade cost him 10¢. Rob's lemonade cost him 20¢.**

6. Whose lemonade was readier to drink when he acquired it?

_____

7. How do you know?

_____

8. Who spent less time fixing his lemonade?

_____

E Cross out the wrong word and write the correct word above it.   (5)

Mr. Casolini owned a grocery store. Last Thanksgiving, he have a big demand for turkeys. People was in the grocery store all day long, buying turkeys. Mr. Casolini were busy all day. When she went home, Mr. Casolini soaked his feet for two hours. His feet hurts from working all day.

F Write a word that comes from **acquire** in each blank. Then write **verb, noun,** or **adjective** after each item.

1. Some people are more _____ than others. _____

2. He _____ a predictable hat.
_____

3. That boat was a cheap _____.
_____

4. Tom is _____ a bunch of flowers for Susan. _____

5. Mr. Chong is very _____.
_____

G Draw in the arrows. Shade in each tube that carries dark blood. Tell what gas each tube carries.

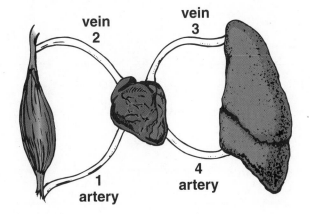

1. _____
2. _____
3. _____
4. _____

H

woman	tree

1. Tell how the objects could be the same.
_____
_____

2. Write a simile about the objects.
_____
_____

1 Underline the redundant sentences.
Circle and correct the punctuation errors.

Gog who was a huge ape was picking his teeth with a pine tree. He had just eaten two million bananas, and bits of banana peel had worked their way between Gog's dainty molars. Gog who was the only ape of his kind in the world had very bad teeth. Gog did not want to go to the dentist; however his teeth felt terrible. There were no other apes like Gog. Gog knew that his dentist, Dr. Painless, would scold Gog for not brushing his teeth more Gog slowly lumbered off to see Dr. Painless. The doctor was going to be mad at Gog. Gog became so afraid that he started to shake, setting off five earthquakes and a tidal wave.

ERRORS	O	W	B	T

A Write the instructions.

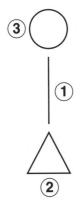

1. _____

   _____

2. _____

   _____

3. _____

   _____

B Rewrite the paragraph in four sentences on your own lined paper.

a. If one of the sentences tells **why,** combine the sentences with **because.**
b. If two sentences seem contradictory, combine them with **however.**
c. Move part of the predicate in sentences you don't combine.

> Another early jazz musician was William Handy. William Handy played the trumpet. Handy's band played in street parades at first. Later, they toured the country. They mostly toured the South. Handy's band was quite different from John Philip Sousa's band. John Philip Sousa's band was also popular at the time.

C Put the statements below the story in the right order.

> Gog, the ape, is having a hard time cleaning his toenails. Yesterday, he played in his sandbox for a few hours, and little grains of sand stuck to his toenails. Last night, he tried to clean his toenails with a toothbrush, but the brush did not work. This morning, he tried a broom, but the broom fell apart. Right now, he is soaking his feet in water, but nothing is happening. Gog is getting desperate because he wants to look good for his date tonight.

A tool fell apart.   _____

A tool did not work.   _____

An ape began to play in sand.   _____

An ape got his feet wet.   _____

Sand stuck to something.   _____

An ape used a sweeping tool.   _____

D Cross out the wrong word and write the correct word above it. **(5)**

Bob likes to play tennis. Him has a good tennis racket. He have good tennis shoes. Bob has everything he needs to play tennis, but Bob can't hit the ball. Him practice every day, but he never wins a game. Sometimes, Bob are sad, but he keeps playing.

E Circle the subject and underline the predicate. Rewrite each sentence by moving part of the predicate.

1. The rivers are low because we've had no rain.

_____

_____

2. Many people can't see without glasses.

_____

_____

3. Janet plays basketball even though she is short.

_____

_____

F Answer the questions.

1. What's the rule about products that are readier to use?

_____

_____

Pam and Sarah got apartments that are alike and that are in the same part of town. Pam's apartment came with a bed, a couch, and some chairs. Sarah's apartment didn't come with anything.

2. Who spends more on rent?

_____

3. How do you know?

_____

_____

Hamburgers you make yourself cost less than hamburgers you get in a restaurant.

4. Which kind of hamburger is readier to use when you obtain it?

_____

5. How do you know?

_____

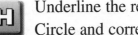

> **Mark works all day and goes to school at night. Jim doesn't work at all, and he doesn't go to school.**

6. Who has more time to work on dinner?

_____

7. Who probably buys foods that are readier to use?

_____

8. Who probably spends less on food?

_____

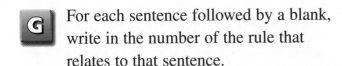 **G** For each sentence followed by a blank, write in the number of the rule that relates to that sentence.

> **1. When the demand is greater than the supply, prices go up.**
>
> **2. Products that are readier to use cost more.**

Beth tried to save money at the supermarket. It was winter, and the store was low on fresh tomatoes, so Beth didn't buy tomatoes. _____ She got regular oatmeal rather than instant oatmeal. _____ She almost got oranges, but oranges were not in season and the store had very few. _____ She got raw beans instead of cooked beans. _____ By the time she finished shopping, she had saved so much money that she bought herself a giant lollipop.

H Underline the redundant sentences. Circle and correct the punctuation errors.

When Gog got to Dr. Painless's office, he told the man, about the bits of banana peel. Dr. Painless sighed and took out his tools. Gog became afraid at the sight of the sharp picks and mean-looking drills. Gog began to shake again. The dental tools scared Gog. He shook so hard that the banana peel bits started to come loose. Now it was Dr. Painless's turn to be afraid Gog's shaking had loosened the bits. Bits were hurtling across the room like rockets. They landed everywhere especially on the dental tools. The picks and drills got covered with bits of peel Gog said, "Gog not afraid of tools anymore. Now tools appeal to Gog."

LESSON 56

I Write a word that comes from **reside** or **acquire** in each blank. Then write **verb, noun,** or **adjective** after each item.

1. She needs to _____ a winter coat. _____

2. Most people prefer to live in _____ areas. _____

3. The _____ of diamonds is a costly hobby. _____

4. Jane wants to _____ in an apartment. _____

5. She is so _____ that her home is bursting with objects. _____

J Make up a simile for each item.

1. They jump very high.

   _____

   _____

2. His beard was very scratchy.

   _____

   _____

K Underline the contradiction. Circle the statement it contradicts. Tell **why** the underlined statement contradicts the circled statement. Make the underlined statement true.

Bob was in a car wreck. Only the nerves that carried messages from his brain to his body were hurt. Bob was very sad. He asked the doctors when he would be well. * The doctors told Bob that he would walk again, but that he might limp. They told him that it would take a year for his sense nerves to heal. Bob stayed in bed for a year and read books.

_____

_____

_____

_____

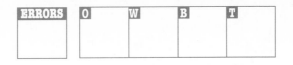
A Put the statements below the story in the right order.

> **Mrs. Lopez was a cook. One day, she decided to make spaghetti noodles. First she made a dough of eggs and flour. She let the dough sit for two hours, and then she pushed it through a pasta machine. The dough came out in long noodles. Mrs. Lopez let them sit for a long time, until they got hard. While the noodles hardened, she made a sauce of meat and tomatoes. She put many spices in the sauce. When the noodles were hard, Mrs. Lopez put them in boiling water. It took Mrs. Lopez all day to make spaghetti.**

She let the dough sit for two hours. _____

She made a meat and tomato sauce. _____

She put the noodles in boiling water. _____

She decided to make spaghetti. _____

She put many spices in the sauce. _____

She made a dough. _____

B Answer the questions.

1. What's the rule about when you buy products in large quantities?

   _____

   _____

   _____

   A man buys 3 pads of paper.

   A big office buys 5000 pads of paper.

2. Who buys large quantities of paper?

   _____

3. Who pays less for each pad?

   _____

4. How do you know?

   _____

   _____

   A big supermarket charges less for

   pumpkins than a small store.

5. Which store probably pays less for each pumpkin?

   _____

6. So which store probably gets its pumpkins in large quantities?

   _____

> **You can buy large quantities of milk from the dairy.**
>
> **You can't buy large quantities of milk from the store.**

7. Where would you pay less for each gallon of milk?

_____

8. How do you know?

_____

_____

_____

C Combine the sentences with **especially.**

1. She worked hard.
She worked hardest in the morning.

_____

_____

2. Days in the desert are hot.
Days in the desert are hottest at noon.

_____

_____

3. Your heart works hard.
Your heart works hardest when you run.

_____

_____

4. The man was mean.
The man was meanest to his dog.

_____

_____

D Underline the redundant sentences. Circle and correct the punctuation errors. Cross out and correct the wording errors.

Tom had a sore trapezius from, reading in bed. He read in bed because the light is not good in his living room. Tom's neck hurt. He did some exercises but it still felt stiff. Tom concluded that he have better stop reading in bed. He bought a lamp at the store and he put it in his living room. Tom improved the light in his house.

E Write the middle part of each deduction.

1. Every plant has roots.

_____

So, a coleus has roots.

2. The museum had paintings by some artists.

_____

So, maybe the museum had a painting by Turner.

3. The museum did not have any paintings by French artists.

_____

So, the museum did not have any paintings by Ingres.

F Write the instructions.

acquire
②

┌─────────────────────┐
│   │
│   │
① │   **trapezius**   │
│   ③   │
│   │
└─────────────────────┘

1. _____

   _____

2. _____

   _____

3. _____

   _____

G Tell **two** ways that the things compared are **not** the same.
Tell **one** way that the things compared **are** the same.

The meat was leather.

1. _____

   _____

2. _____

   _____

3. _____

   _____

H For each sentence followed by a blank, write in the number of the rule that relates to that sentence.

1. **Products that are readier to use cost more.**

2. **When the demand is less than the supply, prices go down.**

   Mr. Bolt manufactured and bottled orange juice. His juice cost a lot more than frozen orange juice. _____ When people started getting low on money, Mr. Bolt's sales dropped. He had to lower his prices. _____ To save money, Mr. Bolt stopped putting real oranges into his juice, and put in just orange flavoring. Mr. Bolt knew that people would still pay more for his juice. _____ And since the juice now cost him less to make, he could still make a lot of money. But people didn't like the way the flavoring tasted. Mr. Bolt's prices dropped again. _____

I Rewrite the paragraph in four sentences on your own lined paper.

a. If one of the sentences tells **why,** combine the sentences with **because.**
b. If sentences seem contradictory, combine them with **although.**
c. Move part of the predicate in sentences you don't combine.

New Orleans was the center of jazz for many years. Jazz musicians played everywhere in the city. They played mostly at dances and in bars. Small jazz bands became very popular. Small jazz bands consisted of a trumpet, a clarinet, a bass, a piano, and drums. The most famous band was King Oliver's band. King Oliver's band had a trumpeter named Louis Armstrong.

J Write a word that comes from **predict** or **acquire** in each blank. Then write **verb, noun,** or **adjective** after each item.

1. Hector fell asleep during the _____ movie. _____

2. That man is _____ that food prices will rise even higher. _____

3. Last week, the bank _____ many stocks. _____

4. An _____ art collector bought all my paintings. _____

5. If a product is popular, you can _____ that its price will go up. _____

K Fill in each blank.

1. _____

2. _____

3. _____

4. _____

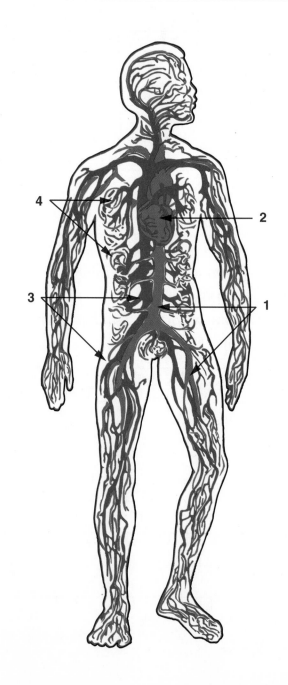

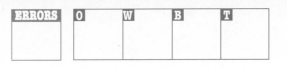

A   Combine the sentences with **especially.**

1. Cats walk quietly.
   Cats walk the most quietly when they are hunting.

   _____

   _____

   _____

2. Her cheeks are red.
   Her cheeks are reddest after she's been outside.

   _____

   _____

3. Their house is dirty.
   Their house is dirtiest after a party.

   _____

   _____

4. Basketball games are fast.
   Basketball games are fastest when the score is tied.

   _____

   _____

B   Answer the questions.   Test #

TOTAL

1. What's the rule about when you buy products in large quantities?

   _____

   _____

   | A woman buys 5 pounds of beef. |
   | A supermarket buys 5000 pounds of beef. |

2. Who buys large quantities of beef?

   _____

3. So who pays less for each pound of beef?

   _____

4. How do you know?

   _____

   _____

   | Mr. Erving pays $125 for each pair of Rocket tennis shoes he buys. |
   | The shoe store pays $35 for each pair of Rocket tennis shoes it buys. |

5. Who pays less for each pair of tennis shoes?

   _____

6. So who buys tennis shoes in large quantities?

   _____

7. How do you know?

_____

_____

> **Store A buys 50,000 cans of King beans.**
> **Store B buys 500 cans of King beans.**

8. Which store pays less for each can of beans?

_____

9. How do you know?

_____

_____

10. Which store could charge less for beans?

_____

 Underline the redundant sentences. Circle and correct the punctuation errors. Cross out and correct the wording errors.

> Blue River flooded because there was a bad rainstorm last night. Water was all over the land. People was riding around their houses in boats. The people got together today and decided to construct a big dike along the river. They will make a big wall next to the river. The dike will cost a lot of money, but they will be worth it

D Underline the nouns. Draw a line **over** the adjectives. Circle the verbs.

1. That man has many useless acquisitions.

2. His older brother is acquiring a new car.

3. Acquisitive shoppers circulated in the mall.

4. The long film had a happy ending.

E Put the statements below the story in the right order.

Rosa and Sue took their vacation in May. They packed their car with clothes and cameras, and then they started to drive to Mexico. On the way, they stopped off in Arizona. The sun was very hot, so they went swimming. They bought some rugs that some Native Americans had made. They ate tacos and hot chili. Then they crossed the Mexican border, and they drove toward the sea. When they found a cozy little hotel beside a sandy beach, they stopped. They stayed at the hotel for a week. They ate good Mexican food and swam in the clear warm water every day.

They ate tacos and hot chili. _____

They packed their car. _____

They found a cozy little hotel. _____

They drove toward the sea. _____

They crossed the Mexican border. _____

They stopped off in Arizona. _____

F Answer the questions.

1. What's the rule about when the demand is less than the supply?

_____

_____

_____

Rose's Toy Shop has 10 baseballs. More than 20 people want to buy baseballs.

---

2. Which is greater, the supply or the demand?

_____

3. What will happen to the price of baseballs?

_____

4. How do you know?

_____

_____

In May, baseballs cost $6 each.

In November, baseballs cost $4 each.

---

5. What happened to the price of baseballs?

_____

6. Which was greater, the supply or the demand?

_____

7. What will the baseball manufacturers try to do?

_____

_____

Name two ways that the manufacturers can do that.

8. _____

_____

9. _____

_____

Last winter, baseballs cost $3 each. This spring, baseballs cost $5 each.

10. What happened to the price of baseballs?

_____

11. Which was greater, the supply or the demand?

_____

G Rewrite the story in six sentences on your own lined paper.

The largest private residence in America is Biltmore House, which is owned by the Vanderbilt family. Although it cost $4 million to build, it is now worth about $65 million. Biltmore House requires a huge staff because it has 250 rooms.

H Use the facts to fill out the form.

Facts: Your name is Julia Rosen. You are applying for a loan. You rent a house at 288 Alder Street, Dallas, Texas, for $400 a month. You work as a clerk for the Dallas Chemical Company, where you make $900 a month. You pay about $80 a month for utilities, $220 a month for car payments, and $30 a month for TV payments.

Instructions:

1. Name: _____

2. Address: _____

_____

3. Check one: own house □ rent house □

4. Employer: _____

5. Position: _____

6. Salary: _____

7. Total monthly payments: _____

8. Subtract line 7 from line 6: _____

I

---
dancer   elastic
---

1. Tell how the objects could be the same.

_____

_____

_____

2. Write a simile about the objects.

_____

_____

---
hair   sunshine
---

3. Tell how the objects could be the same.

_____

_____

4. Write a simile about the objects.

_____

_____

J Write the instructions.

②
acquisition ┃ ①
③

1. _____

_____

2. _____

_____

_____

3. _____

_____

_____

ERRORS | O | W | B | T

A — Answer the questions.

1. What's the rule about products that are readier to use?

_____

_____

2. What's the rule about when you buy products in large quantities?

_____

_____

_____

Liquid milk costs more than powdered milk.

3. Which is readier to use when you obtain it?

_____

4. How do you know?

_____

A grocery store buys larger quantities of canned soup than a person does.

5. Who pays less for canned soup?

_____

6. How do you know?

_____

_____

Lincoln School pays $3 per case of soup.

John's Mart pays $2.50 per case of soup.

7. Which pays less per case of soup?

_____

8. Which buys larger quantities of soup?

_____

9. How do you know?

_____

_____

B Combine the sentences with **especially**.

1. Roses smell good.
   Roses smell best after it rains.

_____

_____

2. Mike eats a lot.
   Mike eats the most when he's tired.

_____

_____

3. Her respiration is slow.
   Her respiration is slowest when she sleeps.

_____

_____

4. The air is dry.
   The air is driest in the winter.

_____

_____

C Fill in each blank with the word that has the same meaning as the word or words under the blank.

1. The man was _____ with money.
   (lucky)

2. She made many _____ predictions.
   (smart)

3. The test was full of _____ questions.
   (not smart)

4. That _____ man hurt his spinal cord.
   (not lucky)

5. Jim's father has been _____
   (not employed)
   for two weeks.

D Circle each bone that will move. Draw an arrow to show which way it will move.

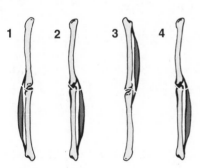

E Rewrite the story in six sentences on your own lined paper.

Egypt and Mexico have many pyramids. Southern Mexico has beautiful pyramids, particularly near Mexico City. Some of these Mexican pyramids are more than a thousand years old, but they are much newer than the Egyptian pyramids.

F Answer the questions.

1. What's the rule about what manufacturers try to do?

   _____

   _____

   _____

   The Fast Eat Shop didn't sell any

   doughnuts last week.

2. Which was greater, the supply or the demand?

   _____

3. What will happen to the price of doughnuts?

   _____

4. What will the Fast Eat Shop try to do?

   _____

   _____

   Name two ways it can do that.

5. _____

   _____

6. _____

   The demand for eggs at the Fast Eat

   Shop is less than the supply of eggs.

7. What will happen to the price of eggs at the Fast Eat Shop?

   _____

8. How do you know?

_____

_____

> **Today, the price of doughnuts went up at the Fast Eat Shop.**

9. Which is greater, the supply or the demand?

_____

10. How do you know?

_____

G Underline the redundant sentences. Circle and correct the punctuation errors. Cross out and correct the wording errors.

Cats purr when they are eating. Cats purr when they is sleeping. Cats also purr when people pet them. Cats purr for many reasons. We don't know how cats purr however we do know which cats can purr, and which cats can't. Small cats, such as house cats and bobcats can purr. Big cats, such as lions and leopards, can't purr. Tigers can't purr.

H Underline the contradiction. Circle the statement it contradicts. Tell **why** the underlined statement contradicts the circled statement. Make the underlined statement true.

Clair had just finished high school, and she wanted to make a lot of money. Because so many people rode bikes, she decided to start making bicycle seats. She made 1000 seats, but nobody wanted them. Clair tried to think up ways to get rid of the seats. * She put ads on television that told how comfortable the seats were. She offered a free pen with every seat. Pretty soon, she had to raise her prices. She started to think that making seats wasn't such a good idea after all.

_____

_____

_____

The _____ is a tube that goes from the mouth to the _____.

1. Fill in the blanks.
2. Circle the word that tells where the tube goes to.
3. Cross out the nouns.
4. Above the first noun, write the name of the body system the sentence tells about.

 Put the statements below the story in the right order.

> **David tried to be a smart shopper. On Saturday, David went shopping. Before he went shopping, David read a consumer report about buying food. When he went shopping, David looked for good deals. He bought grade B eggs because they were cheaper than grade A eggs, but just as good. He acquired a big bag of flour because the big bag cost less per pound. He also bought a big bag of dog food. He obtained raw potatoes because they were cheaper than frozen potatoes. Instead of buying a frozen chicken dinner, David bought a chicken he could fry himself. David paid a lot of money for the food he acquired, but he would have paid a lot more if he hadn't been such a smart shopper.**

He read a consumer report about food. _____

He looked for good deals. _____

He obtained grade B eggs. _____

He bought a chicken he could fry himself. _____

He paid a lot of money. _____

K Follow the directions.

1. Draw a vertical line.
2. Draw another vertical line to the left of the first line.
3. Draw a slanted line from the bottom of the first line to the top of the second line.
4. Above the shape, write the noun that comes from the verb **respire.**

WORD LIST

Acquire (v) *means* get.

Acquisition (n) *means* something you acquire.

Acquisitive (a) *means* that something likes to acquire things.

Conclusion (n) *means* the end or something that is concluded.

Criticism (n) *means* a statement that criticizes.

Demand (n) *means* how well something sells.

Digest (v) *means* change food into fuel for the body.

Erode (v) *means* wear things down.

Explanatory (a) *means* that something explains.

Manufactured (a) *means* that something has been made in a factory.

Motor nerve (n) *means* a nerve that lets you move.

Production (n) *means* something that is produced.

Sense nerve (n) *means* a nerve that lets you feel.

Supply (n) *means* how much there is of something.

A Answer the questions.

1. What's the rule about buying products in large quantities?

_____

_____

_____

2. What's the rule about products that are readier to use?

_____

_____

> **St. Mary's Hospital pays less per head of lettuce than Dr. Green does.**

3. Who buys larger quantities of lettuce?

_____

4. How do you know?

_____

_____

> **Goode Muffins are ready to eat immediately.**
> **Great Muffins are ready to eat in half an hour.**

5. Which muffins are readier to use?

_____

6. Which muffins cost more?

_____

7. If you want to save money, which muffins are better to buy?

_____

8. If you want to save time, which muffins are better to buy?

_____

> **Fran's Cafe buys 50 pounds of chicken each week.**
> **Mick's Diner buys 500 pounds of chicken each week.**

9. Which buys larger quantities of chicken?

_____

10. Which pays less for each pound of chicken?

_____

B Fill in each blank with the word that has the same meaning as the word or words under the blank.

1. Susan was _____ for the
    (not prepared)
pop quiz.

2. Jim concluded that Bob's story was

_____.
    (not believable)

3. She is too _____ to eat.
    (not happy)

4. We were _____ to acquire
    (lucky)
this car.

5. Dick made an _____ selection.
    (not smart)

C Put the statements below the story in the right order.

> **Marta was studying to be a doctor. In her first year of medical school, she learned all about the skeletal system. At the end of the year, Marta was tested on what she had learned. She had to name every bone in the skeleton. Marta named every bone except the upper leg bone, which she couldn't remember. She passed the test anyway, and she began studying the muscular system. In a few months, Marta could name every muscle, and which bone each muscle was attached to. Marta studied all the time, and only went to the movies once a month. Marta knew that she would have to study hard six days a week for the next seven years.**

She did not fail the test. _____

She could name every part of
the muscular system. _____

She couldn't remember what
the femur was called. _____

She was tested on the skeletal
system. _____

She learned all about the system
of bones. _____

She began studying the system
of muscles. _____

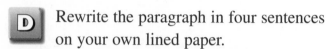 Rewrite the paragraph in four sentences on your own lined paper.

a. If one of the sentences tells **why,** combine the sentences with **because.**
b. If two sentences seem contradictory, combine them with **but.**
c. Move part of the predicate in sentences that you don't combine.

> Louis Armstrong came to Chicago in the 1920s. He started his own band. He began to make recordings. Louis Armstrong's recordings were probably the most important jazz recordings ever made. Louis Armstrong's recordings inspired jazz musicians all over the country. Pretty soon, jazz bands were formed everywhere. Most jazz bands were formed in Chicago and New York.

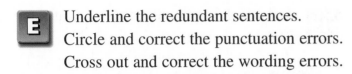

E Underline the redundant sentences. Circle and correct the punctuation errors. Cross out and correct the wording errors.

> Most people likes to play sports. Some people don't. Men what lived thousands of years ago had footraces. They had games, to see who could throw a spear the farthest. They had games to see who could run the fastest. Today, we play basketball football and many other games. People played sports thousands of years ago. People will still be playing and watching sports years from now. There will be sports fans in the future.

F Circle the word that combines the sentences correctly. Combine the sentences with that word.

1. Hector acquired a car.

Hector still rides his bike.

which   because   but

_____

_____

2. That book was predictable.

That book was most predictable near the end.

especially   however   because

_____

_____

3. Tom was going to the party.

His friend Pam was going to the party.

especially   and   which

_____

_____

4. The doctor examined Berta's leg.

The doctor did not look at her femur.

which   although   particularly

_____

_____

_____

5. That young girl participates in many sports.

Her brother participates in many sports.

who   and   although

_____

_____

_____

G Complete the analogies.

1. Tell a part each object has.

   A car is to _____

   as a television is to _____.

2. Tell what each object runs on.

   A car is to _____

   as a television is to _____.

3. Tell what class each object is in.

   A car is to _____

   as a television is to _____.

H Follow the directions.

1. Draw a vertical line.
2. Draw a line that slants down to the right from the bottom of the vertical line.
3. Draw a muscle that covers the right side of the vertical line and attaches to the right side of the slanted line.
4. Draw an arrow that shows which way the muscle will move the slanted line.

I Tell which fact each statement relates to. Make each contradiction true.

> 1. **Canned carrots are readier to use than raw carrots.**
> 2. **When you buy carrots in large quantities, you pay less for each unit.**

a. She bought raw carrots to save time. _____

b. She bought cases of carrots to save money. _____

c. She bought a can of carrots to save time. _____

A Write **R** for each fact that is **relevant** to what happened. Write **I** for each fact that is **irrelevant** to what happened.

Sam bought a big jar of peanut butter.

1. Big jars of peanut butter cost less per pound than little jars of peanut butter. _____

2. Sam has a roommate. _____

3. Sam eats a lot of peanut butter. _____

4. There was a sale on peanut butter at the store. _____

5. Sam likes to make meatballs. _____

 B Answer the questions.

1. What's the rule about products that are readier to use?

_____

_____

2. What's the rule about buying products in large quantities?

_____

_____

_____

The Sport House buys larger quantities of Zip skis than the Winter Shop.

3. Which pays less for Zip skis?

_____

4. Which probably sells Zip skis at a lower price?

_____

John's Sporting Goods pays $50 for each pair of Zip skis.

The Sport House pays $40 for each pair of Zip skis.

5. Which pays less for each pair of Zip skis?

_____

6. Which buys Zip skis in larger quantities?

_____

7. How do you know?

_____

_____

Sue and John shop at the same store. Last night, they both had fried chicken for dinner. Sue's dinner cost $3. John's dinner cost 75¢.

8. Whose dinner cost more?

_____

9. Whose dinner was readier to eat when it was obtained?

_____

10. Who spent more time fixing dinner?

_____

C Write the conclusion of each deduction.

1. Some rock is made of sand.
Marble is a rock.

_____

_____

2. Plants use carbon dioxide.
Poison oak is a plant.

_____

_____

3. Some bones protect body parts.
The patella is a bone.

_____

_____

D Label each nerve.
Write a message for each nerve.

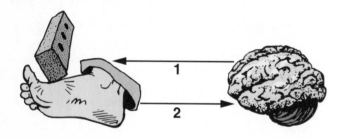

1. _____

2. _____

E Read the story and answer the questions. Circle the **W** if the question is answered by words in the story, and underline those words. Circle the **D** if the question is answered by a deduction.

Mrs. Jenkins runs the only flour mill in Zork City. In October, her mill produces only 1000 pounds, which is half as much flour as Zork City needs each month. Because the demand is so much greater than the supply, she charges $1 a pound for her flour. Mr. Ross thinks that he can make money if he starts another flour mill in Zork City that will compete with Mrs. Jenkins's mill. In November, he puts 1500 pounds up for sale at 75¢ a pound. Everybody starts buying Mr. Ross's flour. Then Mrs. Jenkins, who needs to sell her flour, lowers her price to 50¢ a pound. Everybody starts buying Mrs. Jenkins's flour again. Each mill keeps lowering the price of flour until the price is as low as it can be. This is called a price war, and it always makes consumers very happy.

1. Why can Mrs. Jenkins charge so much for flour in October?

_____

_____

_____ **W**   **D**

2. Which was greater in November, the supply or the demand?

_____ **W**   **D**

3. Why did Mr. Ross sell his flour for less than Mrs. Jenkins's flour?

_____

_____ **W**   **D**

4. What did Mr. Ross do after Mrs. Jenkins lowered her price to 50¢?

_____

5. Flour prices went down in November because of the price war. Give another reason why they went down.

_____

_____ **W**   **D**

6. If both mills end up charging 40¢ a pound for flour, how can one mill attract more customers?

_____

_____

7. Why do price wars make consumers happy?

_____

_____ **W**   **D**

F   Follow the directions.

1. Draw a box.
2. Draw a vertical line from the middle of the bottom horizontal line to the middle of the top horizontal line.
3. To the right of the middle line, print the name of the muscle that covers the back of the humerus.
4. To the left of the middle line, print the name of the muscle that covers the front of the humerus.

G Underline the redundant sentences.
Circle and correct the punctuation errors.
Cross out and correct the wording errors.

Last summer, everybody in Mudville want a pair of sandals. Mr. Jones ran the only shoe store in town. There was a big demand for sandals. Mr. Jones got, lots of sandals from a manufacturer. No other place in town sold sandals. Mr. Jones made one dollar on each pair of sandals that he selling. One day, Mr. Jones selled ninety pairs of sandals. He made ninety dollars from sandal sales that day.

H Rewrite the paragraph in four sentences on your own lined paper.

a. If one of the sentences tells **why,** combine the sentences with **because.**
b. If two sentences seem contradictory, combine them with **however.**
c. Move part of the predicate in sentences that you don't combine.

Thousands of jazz musicians were making recordings and playing concerts by 1930. Most jazz musicians played in big bands. Most jazz musicians also formed small groups. The greatest big-band leader was Duke Ellington. Duke Ellington played the piano. Fletcher Henderson was also good. Count Basie was also good.

I

eyes   steel

1. Tell how the objects could be the same.

_____

_____

2. Write a simile about the objects.

_____

_____

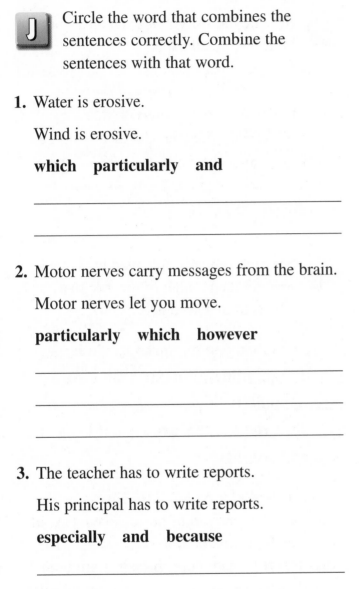

J Circle the word that combines the sentences correctly. Combine the sentences with that word.

1. Water is erosive.

Wind is erosive.

which   particularly   and

_____

_____

2. Motor nerves carry messages from the brain.

Motor nerves let you move.

particularly   which   however

_____

_____

_____

3. The teacher has to write reports.

His principal has to write reports.

especially   and   because

_____

_____

4. She likes to explain her work.

She likes best to explain her painting.

who   especially   because

_____

_____

5. Stars look small.

Stars are big.

who   although   because

_____

_____

A Underline the redundant sentences. Circle and correct the punctuation errors. Cross out and correct the wording errors.

Some peoples read magazines. Some people don't. The store had, many different kinds of magazines John wanted to acquire a magazine, so he go to the store. The store had a wide selection of magazines. John looked, for a magazine about cars. The store had ten different car magazines. John try to decide which one to buy. The store had more than one car magazine. John didn't know which one she wanted.

B Fill in each blank with the word that has the same meaning as the word or words under the blank.

1. Turnips upset his _____.
   (act of digesting)
2. That big old house needs to be

   _____.
   (changed)
3. It is _____ to run on ice.
   (not smart)
4. Susan was _____ for her
   (not prepared)
   camping trip.

5. Bob drew an _____ set of
   (not lucky)
   cards.

C Rewrite the story in six sentences on your own lined paper.

The Great Pyramid, which is one of the Seven Wonders of the World, took years to build. Many people died building the pyramid, especially slaves. Gold and jewels were hidden inside the pyramid for many years.

D For each sentence followed by a blank, write in the number of the rule that relates to that sentence.

| 1. **When you buy products in large quantities, you pay less for each unit.** |
| 2. **Products that are readier to use cost more.** |

Don spends a lot on food. He always gets cooked chicken instead of raw chicken. He only buys a quart of milk at a time. _____ He thinks that if he had more space to store food, he might save money. _____ He thinks that if he had more time to fix dinner, he might save money. _____ Don thinks about saving money a lot, and someday he might do something about it. But until then, he will keep buying frozen dinners. _____

E Answer the questions.

1. What's the rule about buying products in large quantities?

_____

_____

_____

> **Rosa buys 10 loaves of bread a day.**
> **Josie buys 100 loaves of bread a day.**

2. Who buys larger quantities of bread?

_____

3. Who pays less for each loaf of bread?

_____

4. How do you know?

_____

_____

> **Store X charges less for Health Bread than Store Y.**

5. Which store probably pays less for Health Bread?

_____

6. Which store probably buys Health Bread in larger quantities?

_____

> **Cooked potatoes are readier to use than raw potatoes.**

7. Which potatoes cost more?

_____

8. How do you know?

_____

_____

9. If you want to save time, is it better to buy cooked potatoes or raw potatoes?

_____

10. If you want to save money, is it better to buy cooked potatoes or raw potatoes?

_____

F Read the story and answer the questions. Circle the **W** if the question is answered by words in the story, and underline those words. Circle the **D** if the question is answered by a deduction.

Mr. Bock runs the only pen factory in Zork City. Mr. Bock makes his pens very cheaply, and they are not very good. But he can still sell them because the demand is so high. However, Mrs. Flap starts another pen factory in Zork City. Her pens are better made, and they cost the same as Mr. Bock's. Pretty soon, everybody is buying Mrs. Flap's pens. Mr. Bock has to make his pens even better than Mrs. Flap's. People start buying his pens again. Each factory keeps improving its pens until the pens are of top quality. The people of Zork City are very happy, except for Mr. Bock, who liked the early days better.

1. Why weren't Mr. Bock's pens very good?

_____

_____

2. Why did people in Zork City buy his pens?

_____

_____

3. Why did Mrs. Flap make her pens better than Mr. Bock's pens?

_____

_____ **W**   **D**

4. What might have happened to Mr. Bock if he had kept on making the same old pens?

_____

_____ **W**   **D**

5. Car manufacturers always compete with each other. Here are some ways that cars have improved because of competition: better gas mileage, more legroom, disk brakes. Name three more.

_____

_____

_____

6. Name another manufactured product that has improved because of competition.

_____

7. How has it improved?

_____

_____

G Write what each analogy tells.

> **What each object is made of**
> **Where you find each object**
> **What makes each object run**
> **What class each object is in**

1. **An engine** is to **gas**
   as **a light bulb** is to **electricity.**

   _____

   _____

2. **An engine** is to **a car**
   as **a light bulb** is to **a lamp.**

   _____

   _____

3. **An engine** is to **metal**
   as **a light bulb** is to **glass.**

   _____

   _____

H Circle the word that combines the sentences correctly. Combine the sentences with that word.

1. Robin resides in a fancy home.

   Robin acquires many expensive things.

   who   but   although

   _____

   _____

2. People complain about the price of coffee.

   The price of coffee has gone up.

   however   who   because

   _____

   _____

   _____

3. Her heart beats fast.

   Her heart beats faster when she runs.

   particularly   although   and

   _____

   _____

4. The heart works all the time.

   The lungs work all the time.

   especially   and   although

   _____

   _____

5. Some regulations protect consumers.

   Consumers still get cheated.

   which   but   particularly

   _____

   _____

I Underline the nouns. Draw a line **over** the adjectives. Circle the verbs.

1. That smart shopper is buying grain in large quantities.

2. Her older friend participates in many different activities.

3. Those manufacturers are hiring forty new workers.

4. The river has eroded a cave under this cliff.

J Write the instructions.

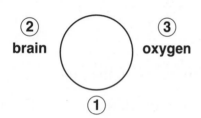

1. _____

_____

2. _____

_____

_____

3. _____

_____

_____

K Make each statement mean the same thing as the statement in the box.

> **The faster the water moves, the more erosive it is.**

1. The faster the water moves, the faster it wears things down.

2. The faster-moving the water, the less it erodes.

3. Things are eroded faster by fast-moving water.

4. The faster the water moves, the slower it wears things down.

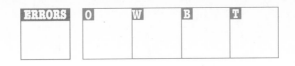

LESSON 63

A Underline the redundant sentences. Circle and correct the punctuation errors. Cross out and correct the wording errors.

Mrs Sullivan was a pencil manufacturer. She made pencils in a factory. Mrs. Sullivan got up at 7 A.M. every day of the week and went to his factory. She even went to work on Sundays. Mrs. Sullivan's factory was clean, and modern Her workers was happy because she paid them a lot of money. Mrs. Sullivan were well-liked, which is rare for a boss. The workers in the factory got good paychecks. They thought Mrs. Sullivan was OK.

B Underline the nouns. Draw a line **over** the adjectives. Circle the verbs.

1. A fussy man rearranged his living room three times.

2. The baseball pitcher considered her next pitch.

3. That shop has rearranged its shelves.

4. Your body digests food and circulates blood.

C Write the instructions.

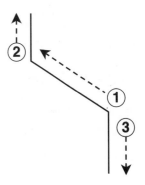

1. _____

_____

2. _____

_____

3. _____

_____

LESSON 63

D Circle the word that combines the sentences correctly. Combine the sentences with that word.

1. The man acquired a lawnmower.

His son acquired a lawnmower.

however   because   and

_____

_____

2. We went backpacking this weekend.

We didn't walk much.

however   particularly   because

_____

_____

_____

3. Some arteries are big.

Arteries are biggest near the heart.

however   especially   which

_____

_____

4. Mrs. Thomas is very rich.

Mrs. Thomas manufactures hospital beds.

although   who   especially

_____

_____

5. Bob was marching in the parade.

Ron was marching in the parade.

and   but   especially

_____

_____

E Make each statement mean the same thing as the statement in the box.

Exercise improves your circulation.

1. Running can make your blood circulate better.

2. The respiration of your blood can be improved by doing sit-ups.

3. If you exercise every day, you will have a better circulatory system.

4. You will improve your digestion if you get a lot of exercise.

F Put the statements below the story in the right order.

> **John hated his life. He worked in a big manufacturing plant in Maryland. Every day was the same. He got up at six o'clock. He got to work at seven o'clock. He punched his time card and had a cup of coffee. Then he stood next to a long belt for eight hours, examining animal crackers. If an animal cracker didn't look like a bear or a lion or a kangaroo, John took the cracker off the belt and threw it away. At five o'clock, when John went home, his wife met him at the door. "I made you a birthday cake," she said. John was surprised. He had forgotten it was his birthday. When his wife put the cake on the table, John fell over laughing. The cake was in the shape of a lion. It looked like a big animal cracker. John picked up the cake and threw it out the window. Then he was sorry and took his wife out to dinner.**

He was surprised. _____

He took crackers off a belt. _____

He threw the cake out the window. _____

He drank some coffee. _____

He and his wife went out to dinner. _____

He got to work at seven o'clock. _____

G Make up a simile for each item.

1. The lawn was soft and flat.

_____

_____

2. The car was big and slow.

_____

_____

H For each sentence followed by a blank, write in the number of the rule that relates to that sentence.

> 1. **Hot air holds more water than cold air.**
> 2. **When hot air rises, it cools off.**

Very warm air blows across the ocean toward the West Coast of the United States. When it reaches the coast, the air is carrying a great deal of water. _____ It is then forced up because of the mountains along the coast. By the time it reaches the mountaintops, the air is quite cool. _____ The air can no longer hold all its water. _____ As a result, there is a lot of rain on the west side of the mountains. When the air goes down the east side of the mountains, it gets warmer. _____

LESSON 63

ERRORS	O	W	B	T

I — Write a word that comes from **acquire** or **participate** in each blank. Then write **verb, noun,** or **adjective** after each item.

1. Soccer is a _____ sport.

_____

2. Mary was selected to _____

in the school play. _____

3. Some people choose to limit their

_____ in sports. _____

4. Jim can't afford to _____

any more shoes. _____

5. A car is an expensive _____.

_____

J — Fill in each blank.

1. _____

2. _____

3. _____

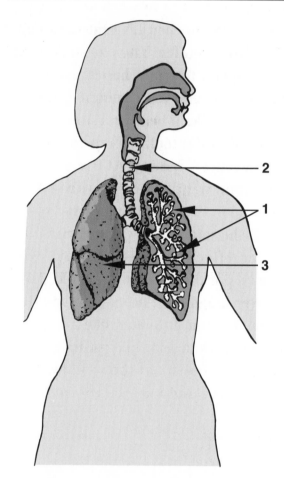

K — Rewrite the story in six sentences on your own lined paper.

German shepherd dogs were first used to protect herds of sheep, especially large herds. Then they were used by the police, who trained them to sniff out criminals. Today, they are used as watchdogs and as guide dogs for the blind.

A Fill in each blank with the word that has the same meaning as the word or words under the blank.

1. The woman liked to _____
(put in order)
flowers.

2. Joe _____ his plan.
(thought about again)

3. That little old man _____
(put in order again)
his checker board.

4. John decided to _____ his story.
(write again)

5. Ron is _____
(thinking about)
getting a new job.

B

<u>**hands   ice**</u>

1. Tell how the objects could be the same.

_____

_____

2. Write a simile about the objects.

_____

C Draw in the arrows. Tell if each tube is a vein or an artery. Tell what gas each tube carries.

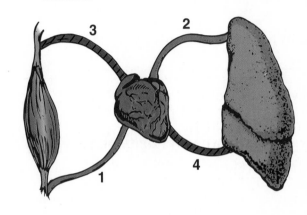

1. _____

2. _____

3. _____

4. _____

D Answer the questions.

1. What's the rule about when the demand is greater than the supply?

_____

_____

_____

<u>**Last year, Johnson's lowered the**</u>

<u>**price of its product.**</u>

2. Which was greater, the supply or the demand?

_____

3. How do you know?

_____

_____

4. What will Johnson's try to do?

_____

_____

Name two ways that Johnson's can do that.

5. _____

6. _____

Johnson's keeps running out of its product now.

7. What will happen to the price of the product?

_____

8. How do you know?

_____

_____

Johnson's manufactures 1000 products a week.

It has orders for 2000 products a week.

9. Which is greater, the supply or the demand?

_____

10. What will happen to the price of the product?

_____

E Put the statements below the story in the right order.

> **Because Henry had worked in construction for many years, he decided to build his own residence. He bought some land in the mountains near a fast-flowing river. He got his friend Burt to help him build. Burt offered much constructive criticism, but he couldn't hammer nails. He kept hitting his fingers. Finally, the house was built and Henry moved in. At night, he could hear the river gurgling and the wind blowing through the pine trees. In the morning, he sat on his porch in the warm sunshine and could see only pine trees, the river, and green meadows. Henry was very happy.**

The house was finished at last. _____

He had worked at building things for a long time. _____

He felt good. _____

He acquired some property. _____

He heard water making noises. _____

He got a pal of his to aid him. _____

He made up his mind to construct his own home. _____

F Underline the contradiction. Circle the statement it contradicts. Tell **why** the underlined statement contradicts the circled statement. Make the underlined statement true.

> Mrs. Jones had a big family, and her husband was unemployed. Her kids loved potatoes, and they ate them every night. Because she didn't have much money, Mrs. Jones always got the cheapest potatoes. Her husband did not participate in the shopping because he was looking for a job. * One night, the family was sitting around eating french fries that Mrs. Jones bought at a restaurant. Mr. Jones said, "I have a big surprise. I got a job today." Everybody was very happy, and Mrs. Jones went to the store to get more potatoes.

_____

_____

_____

G Rewrite the paragraph in four sentences on your own lined paper.

a. If one of the sentences tells **why,** combine the sentences with **because.**
b. If two sentences seem contradictory, combine them with **although.**
c. Move part of the predicate in sentences that you don't combine.

> Many things happened to jazz in the 1930s. The 1930s are also known as the Swing Era. The saxophone became very important. The saxophone could make many new sounds. Many saxophone players became famous. Coleman Hawkins, Lester Young, and Johnny Hodges became the most famous. Many young musicians started playing the saxophone because it was so popular.

H Underline the redundant sentences.
Circle and correct the punctuation errors.
Cross out and correct the wording errors.

The man went from house to house, trying to get peoples to buy cups. People did not need cups consequently, the man wasn't selling very many. The man was a salesperson, but there was no demand for his product. He tried to make people want the cups by telling them that the cups was fun to drink out of. Not many people fell for this line. The man modified, his sales pitch. When he tried to sell the cups, he gave people a different line.

I Fill in each blank.

1. _____

2. _____

3. _____

1 and 3. _____ nervous system

2. _____ nervous system

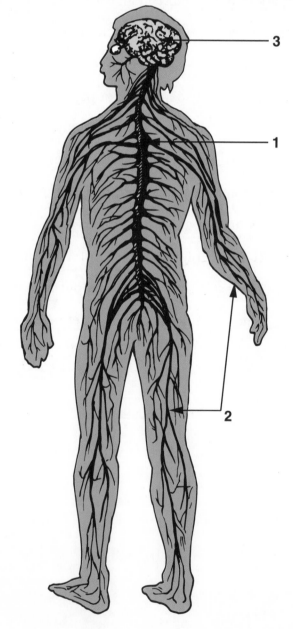

Follow the directions.

1. Print the noun that means **something you acquire.**
2. Draw a horizontal line under that word.
3. Draw a vertical line under the horizontal line.
4. Under the vertical line, print the noun that means **a place where someone lives.**

WORD LIST

Acquire (v) *means* get.
Acquisition (n) *means* something you acquire.
Circulation (n) *means* the act of circulating.
Fortunate (a) *means* lucky.
Intelligent (a) *means* smart.
Protective (a) *means* that something protects.
Redundant (a) *means* that something repeats what has already been said.
Regulate (v) *means* control.
Regulatory (a) *means* that something regulates.
Reside (v) *means* live somewhere.
Respiration (n) *means* the act of respiring.
Selective (a) *means* that someone or something is careful about selecting things.
Unfortunate (a) *means* not lucky.
Unintelligent (a) *means* not smart.

ERRORS	O	W	B	T
			/	

A Underline the contradiction. Circle the statement it contradicts. Tell **why** the underlined statement contradicts the circled statement. Make the underlined statement true.

Fred was a cement producer. He made cement for sidewalks, for new houses, and for driveways. To make cement, he needed lots of sand and gravel. When he ran out of sand and gravel, Fred went to the sand and gravel store. Fred always tried to save money at the store. * The store sold both 50- and 100-pound bags of sand. One day, Fred obtained quite a bit of sand and gravel from the store. He loaded the 50-pound bags into his truck and drove away. The truck was so heavy that it got a flat tire. Fred had never been angrier in his life.

_____

_____

_____

B Rewrite the paragraph in four sentences on your own lined paper.

a. If one of the sentences tells **why,** combine the sentences with **because.**
b. If two sentences seem contradictory, combine them with **but.**
c. Move part of the predicate in sentences that you don't combine.

Billie Holiday was the greatest singer of the Swing Era. Billie Holiday had an amazing voice. Her voice was not very loud. Her voice had great power. Her most famous recordings were made with Lester Young. Lester Young played the tenor saxophone. You should buy some Billie Holiday recordings if you get the chance.

C Follow the directions.

1. Draw a vertical line.
2. Draw a line that slants down to the left from the bottom of the vertical line.
3. Draw a muscle that covers the left side of the vertical line and attaches to the left side of the slanted line.
4. Draw an arrow that shows which way the muscle will move the slanted line.

D Fill in each blank with the word that has the same meaning as the word or words under the blank.

1. The woman _____ her dress.
   (adjusted again)

2. The city is full of _____
   (constructed again)
   buildings.

3. Mary will _____ the
   (put in order)
   basement for her party.

4. Joe _____ his selection.
   (thought about again)

5. The boss _____ his desk.
   (put in order again)

6. Wanda has to _____ her
   (do again)
   homework.

E Read the story and answer the questions. Circle the **W** if the question is answered by words in the story, and underline those words. Circle the **D** if the question is answered by a deduction.

You know that products that are readier to use cost more. Manufacturers know that people will pay more for something that saves time and effort. Linda gets off work at five o'clock. She wants to go to a film at six o'clock, and she also wants to eat dinner. If she fixes dinner at home, she might not make it to the film on time. Besides, she is very tired from working all day and does not feel like working anymore. So she goes to a restaurant. The dinner she gets in the restaurant probably costs three times as much as the dinner she could have fixed at home, but Linda doesn't care. She feels happy that someone other than herself is doing all the work.

1. Why will people pay more for products that are readier to use?

_____

_____

2. Give two reasons why Linda does not want to fix dinner at home.

_____

_____

_____

_____ **W**   **D**

3. Why does the restaurant dinner cost so much more?

_____

_____ **W**   **D**

4. The next day, Linda fixes dinner at home. Give at least two possible reasons why she does that.

_____

_____

5. Who probably spends more on food, a woman who eats out a lot or a woman who cooks?

_____

_____ **W**   **D**

6. Why?

_____

_____

_____

F   Answer the questions.

1. What's the rule about what manufacturers try to do?

_____

_____

_____

> **The Acme Motor Company manufactures 5000 trucks a week. People buy 4000 trucks a week.**

2. Which is greater, the supply or the demand?

_____

3. What will happen to the price of trucks?

_____

4. What will the Acme Motor Company try to do?

_____

_____

> **Name two ways that Acme can do that.**

5. _____

6. _____

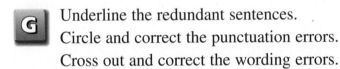

Last year, trucks cost $5000.

This year, trucks cost $4000.

7. What happened to the price of trucks?

_____

8. Which is greater, the supply or the demand?

_____

9. How do you know?

_____

_____

G Underline the redundant sentences.
Circle and correct the punctuation errors.
Cross out and correct the wording errors.

Duke Ellington was the greatest jazz band leader what ever lived. He formed his first band in the 1920s which was when jazz first became popular. Although many of the players changed the band stayed together for almost fifty year. No band leader was better than Ellington. Everybody wanted to play with Ellington; consequently he had no trouble finding the best players. The Ellington band could really swing All kinds of players wanted to belong to it.

H Tell **two** ways the things compared are **not** the same.
Tell **one** way the things compared **are** the same.

Her fingernails are like knives.

1. _____

   _____

2. _____

   _____

3. _____

   _____

MASTER WORD LIST

Abdominal muscle (n) *means* the muscle that goes from the ribs to the pelvis.

Acquire (v) *means* get.

Acquisition (n) *means* something you acquire.

Acquisitive (a) *means* that something likes to acquire things.

Adjective (n) *means* a word that comes before a noun and tells about the noun.

Arrange (v) *means* put in order.

Arteries (n) *means* the tubes that carry blood away from the heart.

Biceps (n) *means* the muscle that covers the front of the humerus.

Brain (n) *means* the organ that lets you think and feel.

Bronchial tubes (n) *means* the tubes inside the lungs.

Capillaries (n) *means* the very small tubes that connect the arteries and veins.

Carbon dioxide (n) *means* a gas that burning things produce.

Central nervous system (n) *means* the body system that is made up of the brain and spinal cord.

Circulate (v) *means* move around.

Circulation (n) *means* the act of circulating.

Circulatory (a) *means* that something involves circulation.

Circulatory system (n) *means* the body system that moves blood around the body.

Conclude (v) *means* end or figure out.

Conclusion (n) *means* the end or something that is concluded.

Conclusive (a) *means* that something is true without any doubt.

Consider (v) *means* think about.

Construct (v) *means* build.

Construction (n) *means* something that is constructed.

Constructive (a) *means* that something is helpful.

Consumable (a) *means* that something can be consumed.

Consume (v) *means* use up or eat.

Consumer (n) *means* something that consumes.

Critical (a) *means* that someone or something criticizes.

Criticism (n) *means* a statement that criticizes.

Criticize (v) *means* find fault with.

Demand (n) *means* how well something sells.

Digest (v) *means* change food into fuel for the body.

Digestion (n) *means* the act of digesting.

Digestive (a) *means* that something involves digestion.

Digestive system (n) *means* the body system that changes food into fuel.

Erode (v) *means* wear things down.

Erosion (n) *means* what happens when something is eroded.

Erosive (a) *means* that something erodes.

Esophagus (n) *means* the tube that goes from the mouth to the stomach.

Examine (v) *means* look at.

Explain (v) *means* make something easier to understand.

Explanation (n) *means* something that explains.

Explanatory (a) *means* that something explains.

Femur (n) *means* the upper leg bone.

Fortunate (a) *means* lucky.

Gastrocnemius (n) *means* the muscle that covers the back of the lower leg.

Heart (n) *means* the pump that moves the blood.

Humerus (n) *means* the upper arm bone.

Intelligent (a) *means* smart.

Irrelevant (a) *means* that something does not help to explain what happened.

Large intestine (n) *means* the organ that stores food the body cannot use.

Liver (n) *means* the organ that makes chemicals that break food down.

Lung (n) *means* a large organ that brings air into contact with blood.

Manufacture (v) *means* make in a factory.

Manufactured (a) *means* that something has been made in a factory.

Manufacturer (n) *means* something that manufactures.

Modification (n) *means* a change.

Modified (a) *means* that something is changed.

Modify (v) *means* change.

Motor nerve (n) *means* a nerve that lets you move.

Mouth (n) *means* the part that takes solid and liquid food in.

Muscular system (n) *means* the body system of muscles.

Nerve (n) *means* a wire in the body that carries messages.

Nervous system (n) *means* the body system of nerves.

Noun (n) *means* a word that names a person, place, or thing.

Obtain (v) *means* get.

Oxygen (n) *means* a gas that burning things need.

Participate (v) *means* take part in something.

Participation (n) *means* the act of participating.

Participatory (a) *means* that something involves participation.

Pelvis (n) *means* the hip bone.

Peripheral nervous system (n) *means* the body system that is made up of all the nerves that lead to and from the spinal cord.

Predicate (n) *means* the part of a sentence that tells more.

Predict (v) *means* say that something will happen.

Predictable (a) *means* that something is easy to predict.

Prediction (n) *means* a statement that predicts.

Produce (v) *means* make.

Production (n) *means* something that is produced.

Productive (a) *means* that something produces a lot of things.

Protect (v) *means* guard.

Protection (n) *means* something that protects.

Protective (a) *means* that something protects.

Quadriceps (n) *means* the muscle that covers the front of the femur.

Rearrange (v) *means* put in order again.

Reconsider (v) *means* think about again.

Redundant (a) *means* that something repeats what has already been said.

Regulate (v) *means* control.

Regulation (n) *means* a rule.

Regulatory (a) *means* that something regulates.

Relevant (a) *means* that something helps to explain what happened.

Reside (v) *means* live somewhere.

Residence (n) *means* a place where someone resides.

Residential (a) *means* that a place has many residences.

MASTER
WORD LIST

Respire (v) *means* breathe.

Respiration (n) *means* the act of respiring.

Respiratory (a) *means* that something involves respiration.

Respiratory system (n) *means* the body system that brings oxygen to the blood.

Ribs (n) *means* the bones that cover the organs in the chest.

Select (v) *means* choose.

Selection (n) *means* something that is selected.

Selective (a) *means* that someone or something is careful about selecting things.

Sense nerve (n) *means* a nerve that lets you feel.

Simile (n) *means* a statement that tells how things are the same.

Skeletal system (n) *means* the body system of bones.

Skull (n) *means* the bone that covers the brain.

Small intestine (n) *means* the organ that gives food to the blood.

Spinal cord (n) *means* the body part that connects the brain to all parts of the body.

Spine (n) *means* the backbone.

Stomach (n) *means* the organ that mixes food with chemicals.

Subject (n) *means* the part of a sentence that names.

Supply (n) *means* how much there is of something.

Trachea (n) *means* the tube that brings outside air to the lungs.

Trapezius (n) *means* the muscle that covers the back of the neck.

Triceps (n) *means* the muscle that covers the back of the humerus.

Unfortunate (a) *means* not lucky.

Unintelligent (a) *means* not smart.

Veins (n) *means* the tubes that carry blood back to the heart.

Verb (n) *means* a word that tells the action that things do.

Write a story about what you see in the picture. Tell what happened before. Tell what is going on now. Tell what will happen. Make your story interesting.

Lessons 1 and 49

Lessons 2 and 50

Lessons 3 and 51

Lessons 4 and 52

Write a story about what you see in the picture. Tell what happened before.
Tell what is going on now. Tell what will happen. Make your story interesting.

Write a story about what you see in the picture. Tell what happened before.
Tell what is going on now. Tell what will happen. Make your story interesting.

Lessons 9 and 57

Lessons 11 and 59

Lessons 10 and 58

Lessons 12 and 60

Write a story about what you see in the picture. Tell what happened before. Tell what is going on now. Tell what will happen. Make your story interesting.

Write a story about what you see in the picture. Tell what happened before. Tell what is going on now. Tell what will happen. Make your story interesting.

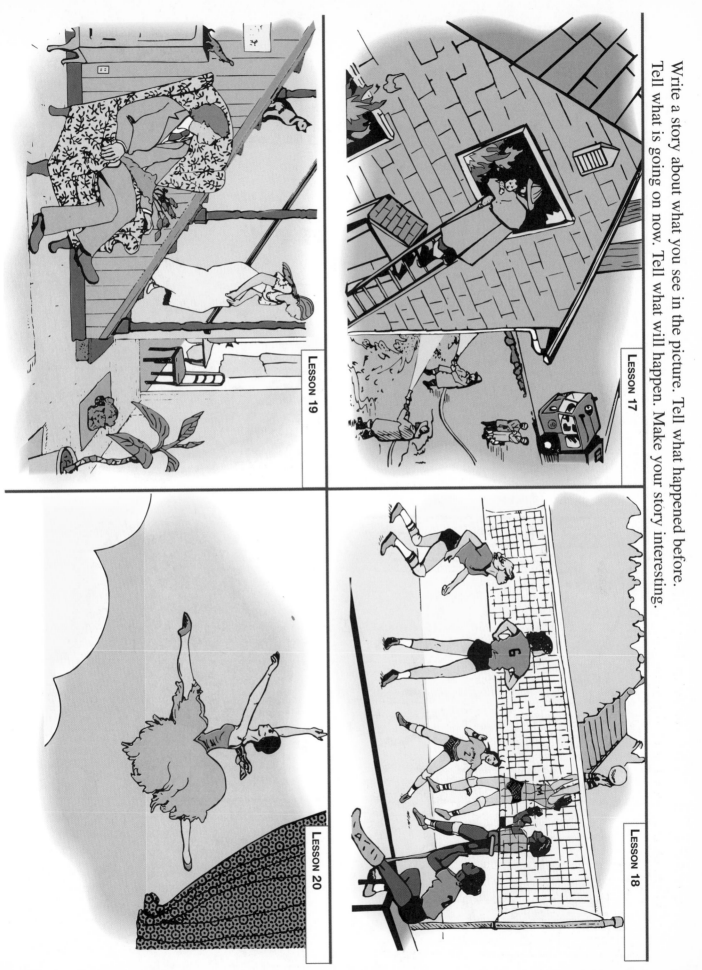

Lesson 17

Lesson 18

Lesson 19

Lesson 20

Write a story about what you see in the picture. Tell what happened before.
Tell what is going on now. Tell what will happen. Make your story interesting.

Write a story about what you see in the picture. Tell what happened before.
Tell what is going on now. Tell what will happen. Make your story interesting.

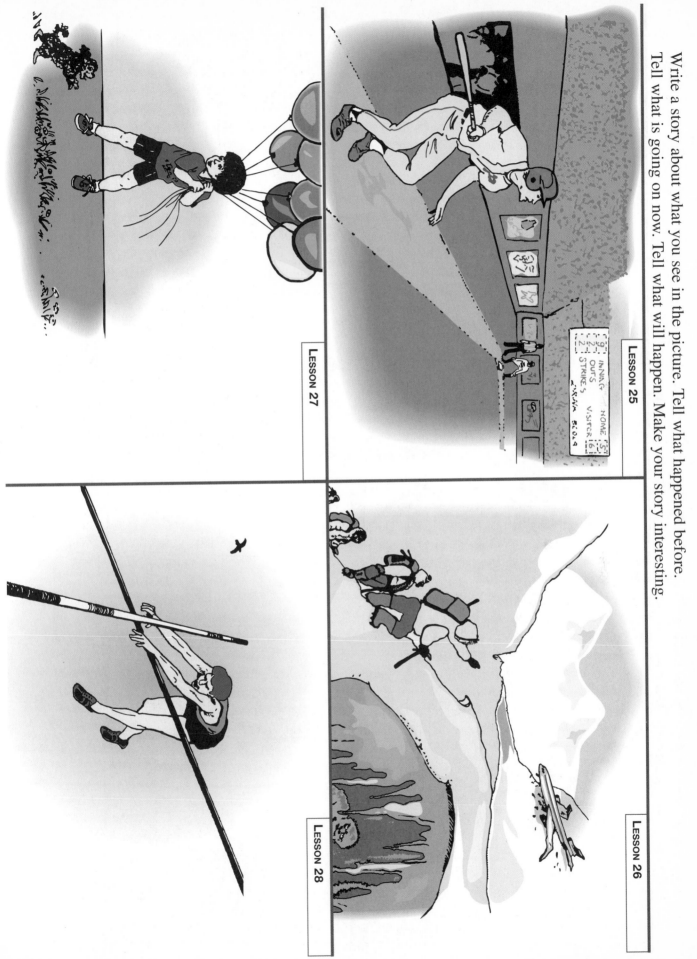

LESSON 25

LESSON 26

LESSON 27

LESSON 28

Write a story about what you see in the picture. Tell what happened before.
Tell what is going on now. Tell what will happen. Make your story interesting.

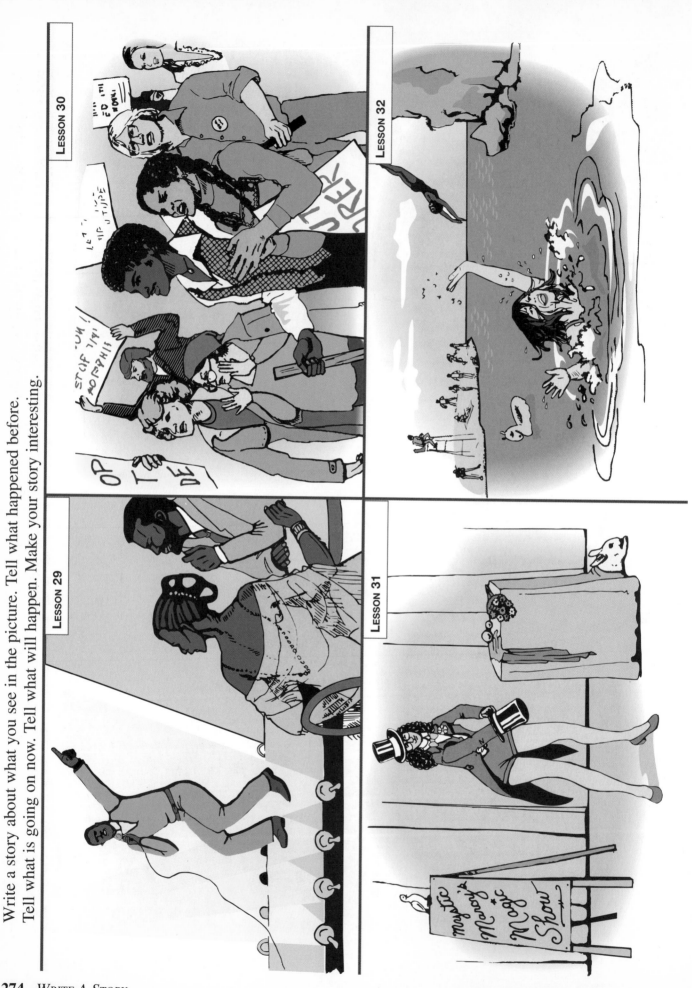

LESSON 29

LESSON 30

LESSON 31

LESSON 32

Write a story about what you see in the picture. Tell what happened before. Tell what is going on now. Tell what will happen. Make your story interesting.

LESSON 33

LESSON 35

LESSON 34

LESSON 36

Write a story about what you see in the picture. Tell what happened before. Tell what is going on now. Tell what will happen. Make your story interesting.

LESSON 37

LESSON 38

LESSON 39

LESSON 40

Write a story about what you see in the picture. Tell what happened before.
Tell what is going on now. Tell what will happen. Make your story interesting.

LESSON 41

LESSON 42

LESSON 43

LESSON 44

Write a story about what you see in the picture. Tell what happened before. Tell what is going on now. Tell what will happen. Make your story interesting.

LESSON 45

LESSON 46

LESSON 47

LESSON 48

COUNTY JOB SERVICE

WALK IN
9:00 - 5:00
MONDAY - FRIDAY

COUNTY JOB
SERVICE

OPEN

1	2	3	4	5	6	7	8	9	10
11	12	13	14	15	16	17	18	19	20
21	22	23	24	25	26	27	28	29	30

FG	MT	BONUS	TOTAL

Fact Game and Mastery Test 1

AFTER LESSON 10

11. a. What do burning things need?
b. What do burning things produce?

3. That old magazine has a large circulation.
a. What are the nouns?
b. What are the adjectives?
c. What's the verb?

4. To breathe cold air can hurt.
a. What's the subject?
b. What's the predicate?

5. Combine the sentences with **because.**
He went running.
He needed some exercise.

6. Name the part of speech for each underlined word.
a. You can <u>digest</u> food more easily if you chew it well.
b. Her <u>conclusive</u> comments changed my mind.
c. His <u>digestion</u> was upset by the bad news.

7. Swimming in that lake is a bad idea.
a. What's the subject?
b. What's the predicate?

8. Name the part of the nervous system shown by each letter in the picture.

9. a. What color is blood that carries oxygen?
b. What color is blood that carries carbon dioxide?

10. Say each sentence using another word for the underlined part.
a. He <u>ended</u> his speech with a joke.
b. She <u>changed</u> the plans for her new house.

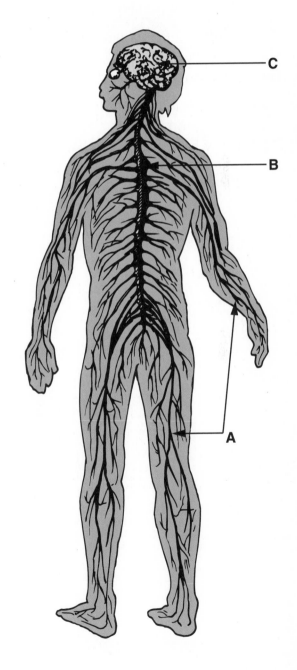

Fact Game and Mastery Test 1

12. Say each sentence using another word for the underlined part.
    a. That office needs many <u>changes</u>.
    b. I didn't like the <u>end</u> of the movie.

13. Combine the sentences with **who** or **which.**
    The triceps has three heads.
    The triceps is a muscle.

14. Combine the sentences with **who** or **which.**
    Frank rides in bike races.
    Frank is my brother.

15. Name the part of speech for each underlined word.
    a. The stomach is part of the <u>digestive</u> system.
    b. Everyone liked the <u>modified</u> book.

16. Combine the sentences with **because.**
    Lynn's femur was broken.
    Lynn was wearing a cast.

17. Name the body system that is made up of nerves.

18. Name the class for each object.
    a. rocket   c. bowl
    b. knife   d. bus

1	2	3	4	5	6	7	8	9	10
11	12	13	14	15	16	17	18	19	20
21	22	23	24	25	26	27	28	29	30

FG	MT	BONUS	TOTAL

3. a. Name the hip bone.
  b. Name the bones that cover the organs in the chest.
  c. Name the upper leg bone.

4. a. What do burning things need?
  b. What do burning things produce?

5. Combine the sentences with **who** or **which.**
His cat ran up the tree.
His cat is one year old.

6. Say each sentence with part of the predicate moved.
  a. He went shopping after work.
  b. His mother has many kinds of plants in her yard.

7. Complete the sentences.
  a. The brain and the spinal cord make up the _____ nervous system.
  b. All the nerves that lead to and from the spinal cord make up the _____ nervous system.

8. Combine the sentences with **who** or **which.**
His cat ran up the tree.
The tree is in the front yard.

9. Say each sentence with part of the predicate moved.
  a. Your circulatory system works hard when you exercise.
  b. She rides horses on weekends.

10. Tell if each tube in the picture carries **oxygen** or **carbon dioxide.**

11. Tell if each tube in the picture is a **vein** or an **artery.**

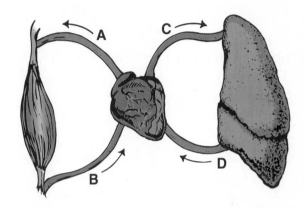

12. Name the part of speech for each underlined word.
  a. Consumers are complaining about the city's water.
  b. Our dog consumed fifty pounds of food last week.

13. Combine the sentences with **who** or **which.**
Pam is a baseball player.
Pam lives in Fulton.

14. Complete each sentence with a word that comes from **consume.**
  a. Caring for three children used to _____ all his time.
  b. This workbook is a _____ product.

Fact Game and
Mastery Test 2

15. Combine the sentences with **who** or **which.**
Fulton is in New York state.
Pam lives in Fulton.

16. Say the whole deduction.
Some planets are very hot.

_____.

So, maybe Venus is very hot.

17. a. What word means **build?**
b. What word means **say that something will happen?**
c. What word means **live somewhere?**

18. Say the whole analogy. Tell what each object is made of.

A **book** is to ____A____ as a **Frisbee** is to

____B____.

FACT GAME SCORECARD

1	2	3	4	5	6	7	8	9	10
11	12	13	14	15	16	17	18	19	20
21	22	23	24	25	26	27	28	29	30

FG	MT	BONUS	TOTAL

3. a. Name the tube that goes from the mouth to the stomach.
   b. Name the tube that brings outside air to the lungs.

4. a. What word means **change?**
   b. What word means **control?**
   c. What word means **look at?**

5. Combine the sentences with **but.**
   Jill was very hungry.
   Jill didn't eat dinner.

6. Complete each sentence with a word that comes from **explain.**
   a. His friends argued about his _____ comments.
   b. My _____ didn't change his mind.

7. Complete each sentence.
   a. The nerves that let you feel are called _____ nerves.
   b. The nerves that let you move are called _____ nerves.

8. Combine the sentences with **but.**
   These chairs cost a lot of money.
   These chairs are falling apart.

9. Look at nerves **A, B,** and **C** in the picture. Tell if each nerve is a **sense nerve** or a **motor nerve.**

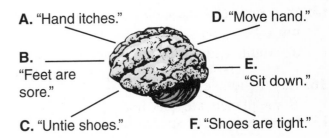

A. "Hand itches." D. "Move hand."
B. _____ "Feet are sore." E. _____ "Sit down."
C. "Untie shoes." F. "Shoes are tight."

10. Look at nerves **D, E,** and **F** in the picture. Tell if each nerve is a **sense nerve** or a **motor nerve.**

11. Say each sentence with part of the predicate moved.
    a. His older brother writes books to make money.
    b. She put on her hat because it was raining.

12. Complete each sentence.
    a. The nerves that carry messages to the brain are called _____ nerves.
    b. The nerves that carry messages from the brain are called _____ nerves.

13. Name the part of speech for each underlined word.
    a. I agreed with his explanation.
    b. This plant is manufacturing toy trains.

Fact Game and
Mastery Test 3

14. Say each sentence with part of the predicate moved.
    a. Nothing can grow on the moon.
    b. My sister stayed up all night to finish the project.

15. Name the part of speech for each underlined word.
    a. She will <u>explain</u> her selection.
    b. These <u>manufactured</u> trees are used in movies.

16. Complete each sentence with a word that comes from **manufacture.**

    a. Her company _____ baseball bats.

    b. That shoe _____ is going out of business.

17. a. Name the body system of bones.
    b. Name the body system of muscles.

18. **A small deer was digesting my lettuce plants.**
    a. What are the nouns?
    b. What are the adjectives?
    c. What's the verb?

1	2	3	4	5	6	7	8	9	10
11	12	13	14	15	16	17	18	19	20
21	22	23	24	25	26	27	28	29	30

FG	MT	BONUS	TOTAL

Fact Game and Mastery Test 4

AFTER LESSON 40

3. Say the whole analogy. Tell what part of speech each word is.

   Participatory is to ____A____ as

   explanation is to ____B____ .

4. Say the whole deduction.
   Some towns do not have a library.

   _____ .

   So, maybe Ashland does not have a library.

5. Complete each sentence with a word that comes from **participate.**

   a. She wanted to _____ in the play.

   b. That school has no _____ sports.

6. Complete each sentence with a word that comes from **circulate.**

   a. News of the party _____ around the school.

   b. Arteries are part of the _____ system.

7. Name the part of speech for each underlined word.
   a. They asked for his participation at the meeting.
   b. Your trachea is part of your respiratory system.

8. Combine the sentences with **particularly.**
   Your circulatory system works hard.
   Your circulatory system works hardest when you exercise.

9. Tell if each statement is about **demand** or **supply.**
   a. The bakery produces 200 loaves of bread every day.
   b. Cars were lined up for gas.

10. Say each sentence using another word for the underlined part.
    a. She moved around among the guests at the party.
    b. He can't breathe through his nose because he has a cold.

11. Say two sentences with the common part. Jessie and Len are going to the party.

12. Combine the sentences with **particularly.**
    Pete watches TV.
    Pete watches the most TV on weekends.

13. Say two sentences with the common part. Doris runs every day because she's in training.

14. Tell if each statement is about **demand** or **supply.**
    a. People buy fewer bikes in the winter.
    b. More new homes were bought last year.

15. Name the part of speech for each underlined word.
    a. They participated in the contest.
    b. Book circulation at the library went up last year.

Fact Game and
Mastery Test 4

16. Complete each sentence with a word that comes from **respire.**

    a. His _____ is very noisy.

    b. She has a _____ illness.

17. Combine the sentences with **because.**
Tom had to cut the grass.
Tom obtained a lawn mower.

18. a. What color is blood that carries carbon dioxide?

    b. What color is blood that carries oxygen?

FACT GAME SCORECARD

1	2	3	4	5	6	7	8	9	10
11	12	13	14	15	16	17	18	19	20
21	22	23	24	25	26	27	28	29	30

FG	MT	BONUS	TOTAL

3. Say the whole analogy. Tell what body system each part is in.

Capillaries are to _____A_____ as

lungs are to _____B_____.

4. A young horse trotted across the green field.
   a. What are the nouns?
   b. What are the adjectives?
   c. What's the verb?

5. Complete each sentence with a word that comes from **erode.**

   a. The ocean is _____ this beach.

   b. Some parts of our state have had lots of

   _____.

6. Combine the sentences with **although.**
   He doesn't exercise.
   He is in good shape.

7. Name the part of speech for each underlined word.
   a. Erosive forces can turn farm land into desert.
   b. They planted grass on the hillside to prevent erosion.

8. In the winter, the demand for ice skates is greater than the supply of ice skates. What will happen to the price of ice skates?

9. Say two sentences with the common part. Eva ran to the store and bought some eggs.

10. Complete the sentence.
   When the demand is greater than the supply, prices go _____.

11. Combine the sentences with **although.**
   She modified her new book.
   Her new book was still boring.

12. Complete the sentence.

   When the demand is less than the supply,

   prices go _____.

13. Complete the sentence.

   Manufacturers try to make the _____A_____

   greater than the _____B_____.

14. In the summer, the demand for ice skates is less than the supply of ice skates. What will happen to the price of ice skates?

15. Say two sentences with the common part. Henry was not feeling well, but he played in the game.

16. In the fall, the price of beach towels goes down. Which is greater, the supply or the demand?

17. a. Name the organ that mixes food with chemicals.
   b. Name the muscle that covers the back of the neck.
   c. Name the upper arm bone.

18. Combine the sentences with **but.**
   This coat was expensive.
   This coat wore out fast.

Fact Game and Mastery Test 6

AFTER LESSON 60

3. a. Name the tubes that carry blood back to the heart.
   b. Name the tubes that carry blood away from the heart.
   c. Name the tubes inside the lungs.

4. Combine the sentences with **especially.**
   She plays basketball.
   She plays the most basketball in the winter.

5. Name the part of speech for each underlined word.
   a. She did not pay much for that acquisition.
   b. She is part of an acquisitive group.

6. Say each sentence using another word for the underlined part.
   a. Her whole family is very smart.
   b. He was lucky to find a job.

7. Store X buys 50 gallons of milk.
   Store Y buys 500 gallons of milk.
   Which store pays less for each gallon of milk?

8. Complete the sentence.
   When you buy products in large quantities, you pay _____ for each unit.

9. Say two sentences with the common part.
   Although she loves to read, she doesn't own any books.

10. Say each sentence with another word for the blank.
    a. I was _____ about my grades.
       (not happy)
    b. He made many _____ comments.
       (not smart)

11. Complete the sentence.
    Products that are readier to use cost _____.

12. Combine the sentences with **especially.**
    Their house seems small.
    Their house seems smallest when they have a party.

13. a. Which is readier to use, raw potatoes or instant mashed potatoes?
    b. So which costs more?

14. Combine the sentences with **however.**
    Whales are not fish.
    Whales live in the sea.

15. Store M pays 25 cents for a dozen eggs.
    Store R pays 40 cents for a dozen eggs.
    Which store buys larger quantities of eggs?

16. Say two sentences with the common part.
    Anna made the trip with Yoko, who is her best friend.

17. Combine the sentences with **however.**
    He bought a car.
    He rides the bus to work.

18. Complete each sentence with a word that comes from **acquire.**
    a. Our team _____ new hats for the game.
    b. He spends lots of money on _____.

FACT GAME SCORECARD

1	2	3	4	5	6	7	8	9	10
11	12	13	14	15	16	17	18	19	20
21	22	23	24	25	26	27	28	29	30

FG	MT	BONUS	TOTAL

3. a. Name the organ that brings food to the blood.
   b. Name the muscle that covers the front of the humerus.
   c. Name the muscle that covers the back of the lower leg.

4. a. What word means **get?**
   b. What word means **find fault with?**
   c. What word means **make?**

5. a. What word means **change?**
   b. What word means **use up?**
   c. What word means **wear things down?**

6. Combine the sentences with **although.**
   Nina and Tina are twins.
   Nina and Tina are not very alike.

7. Combine the sentences with **however.**
   Ron is fortunate with cards.
   Ron lost the game last night.

8. Say each sentence with another word for the blank.

   a. Her father _____ the furniture.
      (set up again)
   b. Bob is _____ modifying his
      (thinking about)
      house.

9. Say two sentences with the common part.
   He cooks lots of curry, which is an Indian food.

10. Say each sentence with another word for the blank.

    a. Henry is _____ a meeting with
       (setting up)
    his boss.

    b. She _____ her plans for
       (thought about again)
    the trip.

11. Say two sentences with the common part.
    They went shopping; however, they have no money.

12. Say each sentence with another word for the blank.

    a. The coach _____ the next
       (thought about)
    play.

    b. Marie _____ the engine in
       (adjusted again)
    her car.

13. Complete the sentence.

    When the demand is less than the supply,

    prices go _____.

14. Complete the sentence.
    Manufacturers try to make the ____A____

    greater than the ____B____.

15. a. Name the upper leg bone.
    b. Name the organ that makes chemicals that break food down.
    c. Name the organ that stores food the body cannot use.

Fact Game and
Mastery Test 7

16. Say the whole deduction.

Some lakes have no fish.

_____.

So, maybe Lake Erie has no fish.

17. Combine the sentences with **who** or **which.**
Boston is on the East Coast.
She is taking the train to Boston.

18. Say the whole analogy. Tell what each word means.

Intelligent is to _____A_____ as

respire is to _____B_____.

FACT GAME 1

3. a. magazine, circulation
   b. that, old, a, large
   c. has
4. a. to breathe cold air
   b. can hurt
5. He went running because he needed some exercise.
6. a. verb
   b. adjective
   c. noun
7. a. swimming in that lake
   b. is a bad idea
8. 1—nerves
   2—spinal cord
   3—brain
9. a. red
   b. (almost) black
10. a. He concluded his speech with a joke.
    b. She modified the plans for her new house.
11. a. oxygen
    b. carbon dioxide
12. a. That office needs many modifications.
    b. I didn't like the conclusion of the movie.
13. The triceps, which is a muscle, has three heads.
14. Frank, who is my brother, rides in bike races.
15. a. adjective
    b. adjective
16. Lynn was wearing a cast because her femur was broken.
17. nervous system
18. a. vehicles
    b. tools
    c. containers
    d. vehicles

FACT GAME 2

3. a. pelvis
   b. ribs
   c. femur
4. a. oxygen
   b. carbon dioxide
5. His cat, which is one year old, ran up the tree.
6. a. After work, he went shopping.
   b. In her yard, his mother has many kinds of plants.
7. a. The brain and the spinal cord make up the central nervous system.
   b. All the nerves that lead to and from the spinal cord make up the peripheral nervous system.
8. His cat ran up the tree, which is in the front yard.
9. a. When you exercise, your circulatory system works hard.
   b. On weekends, she rides horses.
10. A—oxygen   C—carbon dioxide
    B—carbon dioxide   D—oxygen
11. A—artery   C—artery
    B—vein   D—vein
12. a. noun
    b. verb
13. Pam, who lives in Fulton, is a baseball player. or Pam is a baseball player who lives in Fulton. or Pam, who is a baseball player, lives in Fulton.
14. a. Caring for three children used to consume all his time.
    b. This workbook is a consumable product.
15. Pam lives in Fulton, which is in New York State.
16. Some planets are very hot.
    Venus is a planet.
    So, maybe Venus is very hot.

Fact Game
Answer Keys

17. a. construct
    b. predict
    c. reside
18. A **book** is to **paper** as a **Frisbee** is to **plastic.**

FACT GAME 3
3. a. esophagus
   b. trachea
4. a. modify
   b. regulate
   c. examine
5. Jill was very hungry, but she didn't eat dinner.
6. a. His friends argued about his explanatory comments.
   b. My explanation didn't change his mind.
7. a. The nerves that let you feel are called sense nerves.
   b. The nerves that let you move are called motor nerves.
8. These chairs cost a lot of money, but they are falling apart.
9. A—sense nerve
   B—sense nerve
   C—motor nerve
10. D—motor nerve
    E—motor nerve
    F—sense nerve
11. a. To make money, his older brother writes books.
    b. Because it was raining, she put on her hat.
12. a. The nerves that carry messages to the brain are called sense nerves.
    b. The nerves that carry messages from the brain are called motor nerves.

13. a. noun
    b. verb
14. a. On the moon, nothing can grow.
    b. To finish the project, my sister stayed up all night.
15. a. verb
    b. adjective
16. a. Her company manufactures baseball bats.
    b. That shoe manufacturer is going out of business.
17. a. skeletal system
    b. muscular system
18. a. deer, plants
    b. a, small, my, lettuce
    c. was digesting

FACT GAME 4

3. **Participatory** is to **adjective** as **explanation** is to **noun.**

4. Some towns do not have a library.
   Ashland is a town.
   So, maybe Ashland does not have a library.

5. a. She wanted to participate in the play.
   b. That school has no participatory sports.

6. a. News of the party circulated around the school.
   b. Arteries are part of the circulatory system.

7. a. noun
   b. adjective

8. Your circulatory system works hard, particularly when you exercise.

9. a. supply
   b. demand

10. a. She circulated among the guests at the party.
    b. He can't respire through his nose because he has a cold.

11. Jessie is going to the party.
    Len is going to the party.

12. Pete watches TV, particularly on weekends.

13. Doris runs every day.
    Doris is in training.

14. a. demand
    b. demand

15. a. verb
    b. noun

16. a. His respiration is very noisy.
    b. She has a respiratory illness.

17. Tom obtained a lawn mower because he had to cut the grass.

18. a. (almost) black
    b. red

FACT GAME 5

3. **Capillaries** are to **circulatory** as **lungs** are to **respiratory.**

4. a. horse, field
   b. a, young, the, green
   c. trotted

5. a. The ocean is eroding this beach.
   b. Some parts of our state have had lots of erosion.

6. Although he doesn't exercise, he is in good shape.

7. a. adjective
   b. noun

8. It will go up.

9. Eva ran to the store.
   Eva bought some eggs.

10. When the demand is greater than the supply, prices go up.

11. Although she modified her new book, it was still boring.

12. When the demand is less than the supply, prices go down.

13. Manufacturers try to make the demand greater than the supply.

14. It will go down.

15. Henry was not feeling well.
    Henry played in the game.

16. supply

17. a. stomach
    b. trapezius
    c. humerus

18. This coat was expensive, but it wore out fast.

Fact Game
Answer Keys

FACT GAME 6

3. a. veins
   b. arteries
   c. bronchial tubes
4. She plays basketball, especially in the winter.
5. a. noun
   b. adjective
6. a. Her whole family is very intelligent.
   b. He was fortunate to find a job.
7. store Y
8. When you buy products in large quantities, you pay less for each unit.
9. She loves to read.
   She doesn't own any books.
10. a. I was unhappy about my grades.
    b. He made many unintelligent comments.
11. Products that are readier to use cost more.
12. Their house seems small, especially when they have a party.
13. a. instant mashed potatoes
    b. instant mashed potatoes
14. Whales are not fish; however, they live in the sea.
15. store M
16. Anna made the trip with Yoko.
    Yoko is her best friend.
17. He bought a car; however, he rides the bus to work.
18. a. Our team acquired new hats for the game.
    b. He spends lots of money on acquisitions.

FACT GAME 7

3. a. small intestine
   b. biceps
   c. gastrocnemius
4. a. obtain
   b. criticize
   c. produce
5. a. modify
   b. consume
   c. erode
6. Although Nina and Tina are twins, they are not very alike.
7. Ron is fortunate with cards; however, he lost the game last night.
8. a. Her father rearranged the furniture.
   b. Bob is considering modifying his house.
9. He cooks lots of curry.
   Curry is an Indian food.
10. a. Henry is arranging a meeting with his boss.
    b. She reconsidered her plans for the trip.
11. They went shopping.
    They have no money.
12. a. The coach considered the next play.
    b. Marie readjusted the engine in her car.
13. When the demand is less than the supply, prices go down.
14. Manufacturers try to make the demand greater than the supply.
15. a. femur
    b. liver
    c. large intestine
16. Some lakes have no fish.
    Lake Erie is a lake.
    So, maybe Lake Erie has no fish.
17. She is taking the train to Boston, which is on the East Coast.
18. **Intelligent** is to **smart** as **respire** is to **breathe.**